Slow Dancing Is Easy

Scripts for Solo Performer

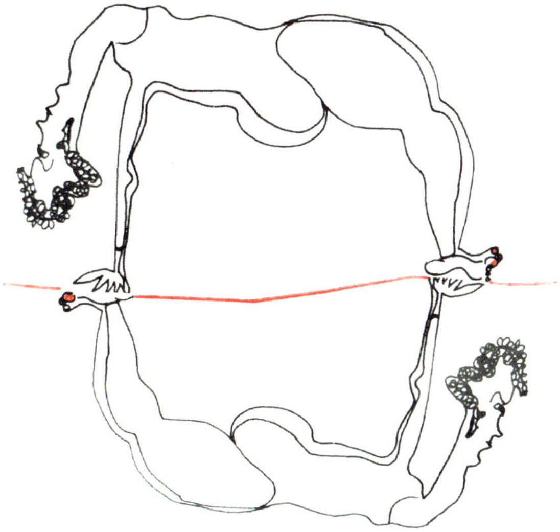

Ara Fitzgerald

Published by Still River Books
[Lincoln, Massachusetts]

ISBN Number: 979-8-9916994-0-2
Library of Congress Control Number: 2024925203

Text and drawings by Ara Fitzgerald
Book design by Ola DeKorne
Photographs by Peter Cunningham

Printed in the United States of America
First published in 2025

www.arafitzgerald.com

TABLE OF CONTENTS

INTRODUCTION

You have in your hands a unique and exciting document of an artist's evolution during many long years of experience.

Ara Fitzgerald is a rare breed of solo performer who writes and performs her own work and continues to hone the work through many long years of performances. She has performed these scripts in theatres, museums, art galleries, Buddhist zendos, festivals, and in living rooms. She is a trained modern dancer as well as an innovative and fearless improviser.

In every performance, whether in her twenties or now in her seventies, Fitzgerald leaps, bends, recites, sings, spins, kicks, and dances Greek myths, recipes, poetry, cats, yoga on the beach, Shakespeare, and personal experiences. She is the ghost of P.T. Barnum as the ringmaster for present-day politics, and questions why Sarah Bernhardt slept in a coffin. With each script and performance, her levity and humor are blended into pathos and truth, offering refreshing and revelatory perspectives on fairy tales, grief, ageing, and so much more.

Slow Dancing is Easy is a book of 15 scripts that Fitzgerald has written, developed, and performed for many decades. The text is accompanied by her own expressive drawings, as well as Peter Cunningham's explosive photographs.

It is a retrospective testament of Ara Fitzgerald's originality and skill. For the general reader, as well as any performer looking for inspiration and guidance, this book is original, powerful, and invaluable.

Dian Parker, *arts writer, R.A.D.A.*

PREFACE

FROM STAGE TO PAGE

I don't remember not dancing. My first performance outside the home was as a duck at age 3 in what must have been a dancing school's *Swan Lake* (abridged). A decade later, given my crooked elbows, full hips and bent for making up new movements in the middle of ballet combinations, my Russian émigré ballet teacher said that although I understood movement, I would never be a ballerina. My world collapsed. Then she kindly added that I might be interested in this thing called modern dance.

At 15, I began to study at the American Dance Festival and for the following seven seasons, including my undergraduate years at Connecticut College, I took class with legends and innovators of the field: José Limón, Martha Graham, Merce Cunningham, Paul Taylor, Alvin Ailey, Bessie Schonberg, Lucas Hoving, Yvonne Rainer, Twyla Tharp, Margie Beals, Meredith Monk, Martha Myers, and Daniel Nagrin. On the stages of those days, to distinguish itself as a serious art form, the evolving modern dance field, for the most part, did not include the spoken word, celebrating movement as its primary language.

I, however, was a walker and a talker. The granddaughter of a vaudevillian. Dance and theater were bred in my bones. An improvisor. In the 1970s, I joined Daniel Nagrin's Workgroup whose improvisations were inspired by the investigations of Joe Chaikin's Open Theatre. When exploring the breath, rhythms, and interplay of particular images or questions, I felt like I was being danced, rather than willing my body to perform perfections in space and time. I found my artistic home.

In 1980, I began to include language in performance. Composer Wall Matthews and I collaborated on *Words for Music Perhaps* based on the Crazy Jane poems of William Butler Yeats. The integration of poetry, music and dance grew organically in our process and inspired me to begin to create text for solo performance. Here they move from stage to page.

Cavorting in beginner's mind, the drawings in the book emerged intuitively, marks on a page, another kind of improvisation.

As I age, I pick up puzzle pieces of experience and observation that link a life story. Aspects of memoir inform the pieces. See *Notes on the Pieces* at the end of the book for prompts and background stories. I can imagine the pieces being adapted and performed by others. Please reach out to me for permissions.

Decades ago, when I told my grandmother, the one who led the St. Louis Syncopators, an 'all-girl' jazz band, on the vaudeville circuit, that after graduation from college, I would pursue modern dance, she chortled, "A modern dancer is just a vaudevillian with an education." I can still hear her laugh.

Ara Fitzgerald

PART I

ON LOOKING BACK

First Recipe

FIRST RECIPE (2009)

I'm thinking.
I'm thinking of eating.
Are you?

Ummmm.... I'm thinking of recipes.
So many recipes.
Recipes for cooking things up.

I think of my mother.
Recipes from my mother
handed to her from her mother, and her mother from her mother and back and back
and back, and back and back and back...

My two grandmothers:
One followed recipes exactly and the other was a vaudevillian
with a jazz band who improvised while she cooked.

A little of this and a little of that
a dab here
and a dash there
a sprinkle, a sprinkle, a sprinkle, sprinkle, sprinkle—
to taste to taste, to taste, to taste to taste.
Oh!
And a bunch of these and a hunk of that
and a bake, a bake, a bake, a bake, a bake.
And before we knew it
—5, 6, 7, 8—
we had a deep dish, a deep dish, a deep dish apple pie.

I'm thinking there must have a been a first recipe.
What was the very first recipe?
Go back. Mother to mother. Keep going back, further —
mother to mother to mother to mother, and some fathers.

Families gather around food.

Oh.
A man. A woman. A recipe.
First Woman. First Man. First Recipe.

I'm thinking of the Garden of Eden.
Are you?

First Recipe.
Assemble ingredients:

1 ripe red apple
1 Adam
1 Eve
1 serpent
2-4 fig leaves
Season with temptation.

To Prepare:

Knead one 12 lb. jeweled serpent 'round a fresh green branch
of that old apple tree.

Let rest until Eve appears and the serpent begins to rise.

Infuse with temptation to taste.

Seduce with nutrients of knowledge.

Pay no attention to Eve's protests,
"Thank you, thank you. Thank you! And no thank you!
I will die if I bite your apple and I'm not hungry anyway."

She's just being polite.

Meanwhile, marinate overnight while Eve makes up her mind.

"Yes, no, yes, no, yes, no…"

"SSSSS." When the hissing stops,
ask Eve again if she would like a teeny tiny test taste.

"There's nothing to lose."

Let rest again, five minutes, or until she says, "Yes!"

and calls, “Adam! Come and get it!”

When Adam appears

Rinse fig leaves.

Pat dry.

Allow nature to take its course.

Toss fig leaves to Adam and Eve as they exit paradise, stage right.

My grandmother would call this ‘the fatal nosh.’

Today we are no longer tempted by apples.
We are seduced by snack attacks of Biblical portions.

Today’s serpents offer us
supersize sodas, bushels of fries, and bottomless big box pies.
Fillers and lies disguised as ‘nutrients’ that tempt but never satisfy.

Watch carefully as we waddle out of paradise, stage right.

AS IT TURNS OUT, **INVISIBILITY** SERVES MY **CURIOSITY.**

THE CHOCK FULL O'NUTS ORACLE (2017)

I'm 25 years old.
No, not now.
It is 1972.
I sit at the Chock full o'Nuts counter savoring a nutted cheese sandwich
(cream cheese between two slices of date nut raisin bread)
advertised in its preparation as untouched by human hands.
This sandwich is affordable and delicious.
I am 25 years old. I am living in New York City.
I am happy.

A woman, older than me, maybe fifty.
a bit unkempt,
plops down on the stool to my left,
stares at me and without introduction snarls:

"One day you'll see!
You just wake up, look in the mirror and suddenly you're old.
Everything falls down all at once.
Your looks will be gone.
Pfttt.... just like that!
Boom!"

She makes an impression.

In silence I eat my sandwich and contemplate the future.
I wonder if her bitter description of the sudden fall into old age
will come true.
At least I've been warned.
I thank her for sharing.

It turns out, my life is not nearly as drop-down horrific as she predicted.
I remember her as about fifty and now the fifties are my younger years.
Aging of the body has been steady, not sudden,

and mind and spirit remain free of temporal shenanigans, for the moment.

It's a relief to be past the focus on youthful skin.
I am wrinkly. I am living in New York City.
I am living! And I am happy.

I remember the moment I became invisible.

It is 1992. I am 45 years old.

I walk into a bar in Hartford, Ct.
with a cast member following a rehearsal of *A Doll's House*.
I am aware that with the exception of my friend,
no one else registers my human presence.
They cannot see me.
I no longer exist in their eyes.

I come from a generation when construction workers
routinely spewed moist kissy kissy catcalls
to young women as they walked past.
At work by the copy machine
there could be a sudden pinch on the butt for no good reason.
No explanation, no apology.
Apparently, some of this still goes on.

Noticing not being noticed at age 45,
I remember that moment
at the lunch counter eating a nutted cheese sandwich
contemplating the prediction of the Choc full o' Nuts Oracle.

As it turns out, invisibility serves my curiosity.
I can watch interactions between people and not be noticed.
I can stare with impunity.
I decide that invisibility,
rather than a loss, is liberation.

An I-Thou Kind of a Guy

AN I-THOU KIND OF A GUY (2014)

I never saw *Cats*, the musical, on Broadway
or in any high school or elementary school auditorium.
I hadn't read T.S. Eliot's *Old Possum's Book of Practical Cats*
as a child or to my children.

So, later in life, I delighted in Eliot's poem,
The Naming of Cats,
because decades ago, I and then we,
had two cats with three names.

They danced into our family.

One of them was a magical cat,
a mystical cat, a perfect being
with a comically expressive golden tail.
As I have come to learn,
no perfect being lacks a sense of humor.

It is 1978.
After a long day of teaching
I stumble into the living room of the O'Neill Theater Center
where faculty gather before dinner.
The director of the program and the music director
each cup a tiny kitten in their hands.
They lift them up, wiggle them gently in a unison dance
and say, 'Oh, Ara, look at these Irish kitties!'

Because of my last name, people think I am more Irish than I am.
The directors enact the verb 'entice'
in this scene with kittens, abandoned on the porch
of the main building we call the mansion.
Kittens in need of adoption.

One of these fluffy white kittens
has a black spot between her ears
three tastefully placed black dots on her back
and a matching black tail
which she wags with nonchalance and cool confidence
like she knows that she will grow up
to be permanently dressed
in the perfect black cocktail dress.
She is by nature remote.

The other one sports spots of golden fur between his ears
and splotches of gold on his body.
With curiosity and abandon,
he curls and uncurls that comically expressive tail.

He looks me square in the eye.
He seems to be laughing.
His gaze—not the male gaze— the cat gaze:
real, deep, pure, adorable, Egyptian.

Instantly I adopt them.
Or am I adopted?
Am I adopted?

I call my mother.

She lives on Captain's Walk
—once called, simply, State Street—
near the train station to which
I commute once a week from New York City.

Neither of us has much money.
To save on taxi fare, she lends me her old pink car,
a Rambler—we had Ramblers then—
to drive the 20 minutes to the O'Neill Theater Center.

When I tell her I've adopted or been adopted by two kittens,
she says, "Oh, sweetie, I have pretty much given up hope
of ever having grandchildren,
so I accept the substitute of these dear kittens.
I'll get a box with a cover so you can carry them back to New York."
She is even sweeter than this sounds
and she always makes me laugh.

Reminder: it's 1978— pre-seat belts and warnings about distracted driving.
I open the pink Rambler car door just a crack,

slip the kittens in and scoot in before they can escape.

On the drive back to New London,
the kitties MEOW/HOWL.
I purr like a Mama cat and coo,
"It's OK. It's all going to be OK.
You are going home."

The kittens race about the old car
and occasionally dash under the clutch.
I drive to New London, giggling and unafraid.

My boyfriend, soon to be my first husband,
and father of our two sons,
muses with me about names.
Luckily, he turns out to be a cat lover.
"They must have a first, middle, and a last name!"

Hmm…the black and white one is by nature remote,
not a traveler to the human world.
She is a cat, just a cat, and a beautiful cat at that.
Like Audrey Hepburn playing a cat.
Or like a rose. Just like a rose.

Her name.
First name: Rose.
Last name: Rose.
Middle name: Just.
Rose Just Rose.
A rose is a rose is a rose.
Rose Just Rose.

But the other one,
he has something— a presence.
He seems to see into us.
He speaks across the cat/human divide.
He is an I/Thou kind of a guy.

Of course!
Last name: Buber, as in Martin Buber.
First name: Gladstone, as in Eugene O'Neill's middle name
Middle name: the initial E, just E as in Eugene.

Gladstone E. Buber.
Beloved by all who know him.

For 13 years Gladstone E. Buber is a hep city cat.
He lives indoors with Rose Just Rose.

He lounges in the sun on the windowsill,
scampers up and down the living room,
somersaults stoned on catnip
and chases his tail in circles.

He never meets a bird or a dog, grass, trees,
wind or the outdoor sun.
The most wildlife he encounters is the occasional mouse.

But in his later years, the family moves.

Surviving his second car ride,
Gladstone E. Buber meditates
as the van door slides open,
the fancy orange cat carrier door opens,
the door to the house opens.

Three doors have opened.
He continues to contemplate.

Rose Just Rose takes one look at the big bad outdoors,
beelines from the car to the house
and finds solace behind the living room couch
where she spends most of the remainder of her life,
falling over dead on the kitchen floor
on her way to breakfast at the age of 17.

Back to Buber.
He sits at attention in the car in the driveway of the new house.
He continues to meditate on the three open doors
and with cautious curiosity slowly slinks
from the van to the ground
of this wild place— the suburbs of New York City.

He has never seen grass.
He stalks the grass. "It wiggles but it's not a mouse."
He stalks again. "It wiggles but it's not a mouse."

Ah, sweet grass!
Never again the smelly humiliation of a cat box for Gladstone E. Buber.

Tail high, he saunters into the very old house— his estate—
with three floors and an outdoors,
with nearby fields for mouse expeditions and meeting up with chipmunks.
When it's time to go out, a simple "Meow!" opens the back door
and the children stop pulling his tail.
Or with a more plaintive "Meow!!"
They put him down after taking turns parading around the house,
Buber wrapped around their necks
like a woolly scarf or a magic cape.
"Meow!!!" and he's put down,

"Meow!" and the back door opens.
The children do love him so.

Our friend, a Norwegian potter,
sits at the kitchen table.
She drinks milk from a wine glass.
Buber silently hops up on the kitchen table
and watches her.
She takes a sip, returns the glass to the table.
Enraptured, he gazes lovingly at her
and then carefully, elegantly,
dips his paw into her wine glass.
She smiles. Buber dips again.

I/Thou milk. I/Thou glass. I/Thou woman and cat.
Everyone thinks Buber loves them best.
And he does, of course.

Years later, when Buber would have been nearing 100 in cat years,
our friend asks in a letter —we had letters then—
how he is doing. She misses him so.

At 16, in human years,
an inoperable tumor protrudes over his right eye.
Buber meows faintly to go outside.
He leaves the house,
lilting side-to-side,
slight happy flick of the tail but no scamper.
He does not return.
We, his family, cannot find him.

Together we decide he has chosen
a welcoming soft place
under a pine tree or hidden
in tall sweet grass
to rest quietly and embrace death.

"It wiggles but it's not a mouse."
This wise guy, so full of life's joy.

Does a dog have Buddha nature?
"Mu?"
"Meow!!"

It was a cat with three names all along.

Dog Day Ditto

From *The Adventures of The Ever-Fragmenting Woman* (PG-35)

DOG DAY DITTO (1994)

Narrator: The Ever-Fragmenting Woman drove down the highway to work.
The Ever-Fragmenting Woman drove down the highway to work.
The Ever-Fragmenting Woman drove down the highway to work.
She was not:
A. Writing an Academy Awards acceptance speech.
B. Writing her second novel after giving up a prestigious op-ed column at the paper of record.
C. Secretly dating Brad Pitt.
D. Lying in a Land's End hammock, nestled between two scrub pines somewhere near the sea.
The Ever-Fragmenting Woman drove down the highway to work.
She was doing 65 and using her peripheral vision.

(EFW, The Ever Fragmenting Woman, parks the car and enters a classroom.)

EFW: Good morning, class! Today is March 3, 1994
And we will study
past... present... and future....
For instance—
Did you hear the school band playing?
Do you hear the school band playing?
Will you hear the school band playing?

Eight Year-Old: OOoo... ..I know, I know!
The answer is No. No. I dunno.

EFW: Not quite. Could you share with us, please,
how you got those answers?

Eight Year-Old: Sure. Listen carefully... please...
Did you hear the school band playing?
No!
Do you hear the school band playing?

No!
Will you hear the school band playing?
I dunno.

EFW: I see.
Before. During. And after.
Past. Present. And future.
For instance:
What did you do yesterday?

Eight Year-Old: Nothin'...

EFW: What are you doing now?

Eight Year-Old: Nothin'...

EFW: What will you do tomorrow?

Eight Year-Old: Well, I dunno.

EFW: Okay. Let's try this. Turn to the worksheet on page 34. Notice the picture of the vet with the dog. Do you see the bandages? That's what's going on now—in the present—in the picture. I want you to make up a story about the picture of the vet with the dog and the bandages. I want you to think about what happened before and what will happen after—the picture of the vet wrapping the paw of the dog. What happened before? What's going on now? And what will happen after? Use your verbs and your tenses. Make sentences for before, during, and after. Two sentences for each. Go!

Eight Year-Old: The car ran over the dog.
The dog lay on the ground thinking of death.
The veterinarian is helping the dog get better.
The dog doesn't have a clue what's going on.
The dog is (will be) getting better.
The dog has (will have) a clue what's going on.

EFW: That's coming!

Eight Year-Old: Mrs. Fragment!
My dog definitely has a clue what's going on.
My dog does dittos! Watch!
The first skyscraper was invented:
A. To get closer to the sun.
B. So people could work on top of each other.

C. Because there was no more room to go sideways.
D. Opposable thumbs.

Dog: *(thinking, then panting audibly the answer.)*
Opposable thumbs, opposable thumbs!

Eight Year-Old: The fact that John Adams and Thomas Jefferson
both died on the 4th of July:
A. Means they were both born on the same day.
B. Means they planned it that way.
C. Means nothing.
D. Opposable thumbs.

Dog: Opposable thumbs, opposable thumbs!

Eight Year-Old: The war was caused because:
A. The archduke was angry.
B. The people couldn't get any potatoes.
C. Opposable thumbs.
D. The ship blew up.

Dog: OH, ruff, awwgrnnnn ohhhh, there's always a pattern to these things... cause and effect, cause and effect, cause and effect.... Opposable thumbs! I would just like to say that what I really think is going on here is opposable thumbs. The short first digit of the human hand, opposable to all the others. A tool. Not a paw! Aw, awwwwruff, ruff...

EFW: He has a point. I think we should welcome him to class.
Welcome!
That will be all for today, class.

Narrator: The Ever-Fragmenting Woman drove down the highway from work.
The Ever-Fragmenting Woman drove down the highway from work.
She was not:
A. Appearing before a senate subcommittee.
B. Performing open heart surgery.
C. Secretly dating Brad Pitt.
D. Floating on a raft in Tahiti.
The Ever-Fragmenting Woman drove down the highway from work, and flipped the G.D. minivan five F***ing times!

EFW: Watch the glass breaking.
Watch the sunlight on the glass breaking.
Watch the sunlight on the beautiful, shatterproof glass breaking.

Narrator: From the story you can tell
that the shatterproof glass:
A. Won't break.
B. Isn't sharp.
C. Will cost a lot of money.

Birds that land in the same direction as the wind are:
A. Likely to fall sideways.
B. Likely to overshoot the landing spot.
C. Likely to undershoot the landing spot.

An octopus, when it is the same color as its surroundings:
A. Is happy.
B. Is upset.
C. Is dead.

EFW: Just watch the beautiful glass breaking. Watch
the sunlight on the beautiful, shatterproof glass breaking—
putting everything in perspective.

Narrator: The newly awakened shouldn't use their:
A. Heads right away.
B. Arms right away.
C. Legs right away.

From the story you can tell that fish:
A. Learn something very slowly.
B. Learn something very fast.
C. Can't learn anything at all.

EFW: The children still see angels.
Take care of the jumping children.
All the jumping children.
Take care of the jumping children.
All the jumping children.

Narrator: Do you hear the school band playing?

EFW: Yes. I hear the school band playing,
in all its beautiful dissonance.

Sounds of an out-of-tune school band which the EFW conducts.

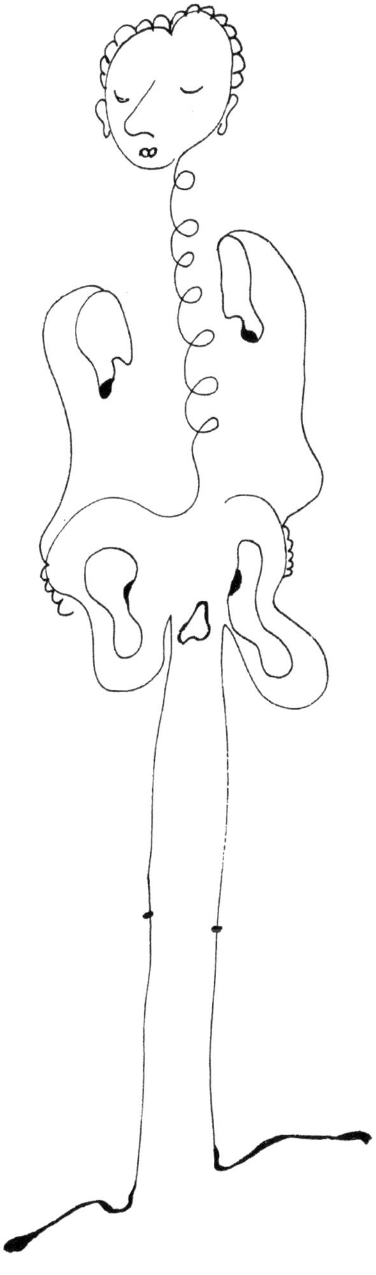

Yoga Beach

YOGA BEACH (1996)

The Ever-Fragmenting Woman decided to go on vacation.

(Mountain Pose)

But first she had to buy a bathing suit.

(Eagle to Triangle Pose)

The first one she tried on had a little skirt that swirled out from the waist. It said, “I should go down to your knees but I don’t. You should go in the water, but you won’t.” She said, “No, thank-you.”

(Downward Facing Dog)

The next one she tried on was gold lamé, and cut all the way up to the iliac crest, totally exposing hips and thighs.

(Plank)

She knew she could no more have those buns iced and baked in time, anymore than she could be a stand-in for Demi Moore.

(Crescent Moon)

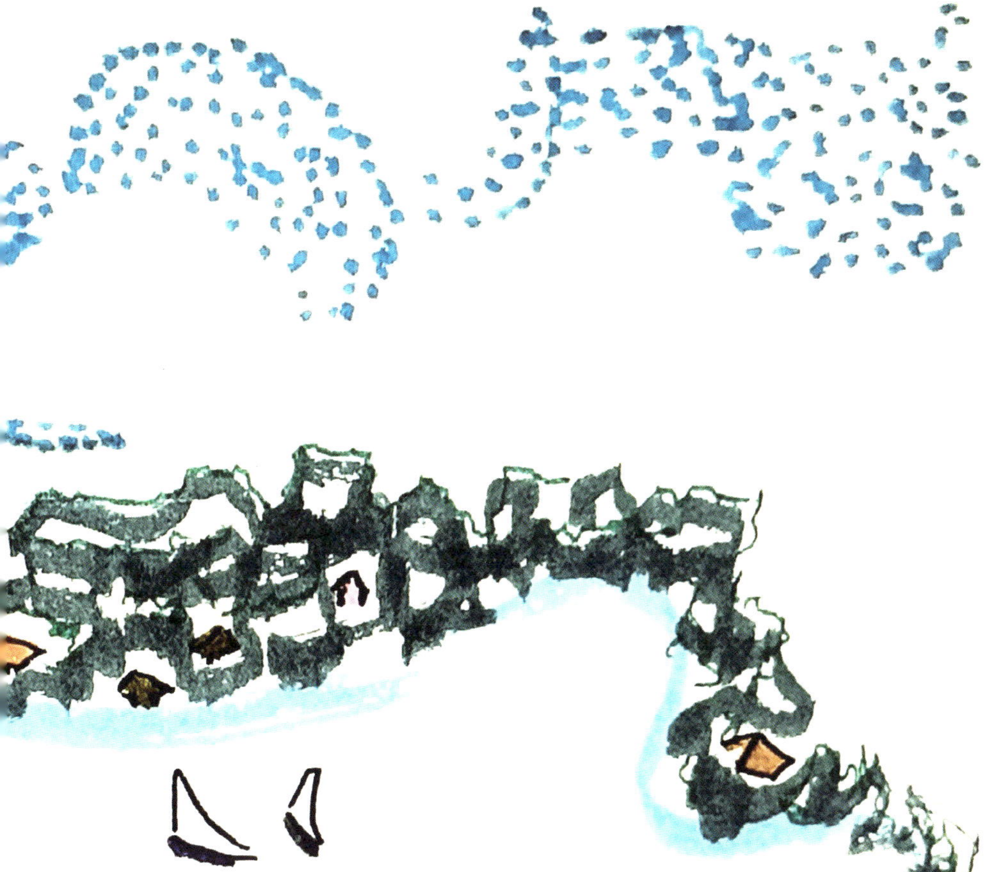

Then, she nearly fell down memory lane in a bikini.
But came to her senses in a rip-off of a Speedo— ‘One-size-fits-all.’

She briefly considered going to the beach in her underwear but decided against it for the sake of the children.

(Child Pose to Rag Doll to Racing Dive)

Then, she nearly fell down Memory Lane in a bikini,
but came to her senses in a rip-off of a Speedo, ‘One-size-fits-all.’

(Sits in her folding beach chair)
Looks great under a towel.

(Upside down in the beach chair)

She was at peace in all the particulars. She had stopped running. This moment was life enough. When all of a sudden she heard... “AGHHH, Ahh, AGHHH, AGHHH OHHooooo-” huffing and puffing behind her. And she turned to see a woman about her own age, chest heaving, wearing a real Speedo who said, “You’ll have to move on. This is a private beach!”

EFW: But I didn’t see any signs!
(Aside to self: This one couldn’t be my fault.)

Woman: AHHK, they keep taking them down!

EFW: Oh, I guess you must be the woman
who lives in that big house up the steep wooden stairs at the top of the dunes.

(Headstand)

Woman: Why, yes I am. Tell me, do you rent or own?

EFW: What?

(Seated Spinal Twist)

Woman: Do you rent or own?

EFW: What?

Woman: Oh, dear. Because. Well, you look like someone who can understand. I’m sure you will understand. This has nothing to do with you. But I mean how would you like it if people just traipsed across your front lawn, sat down, and had picnics there?

(Tree Pose)

EFW: (Aside to self: Detachment, Va-ca-tion... Don’t get reeled in.... Let her go.)

I’d be happy to move on.

(Packs up her beach chair, beach bag and Yoga mat.)

Woman: Thank you for understanding. I’m so relieved.
I just knew you’d understand. I just knew it!

(Moves on. Sets up down the beach.)

EFW: She was at peace in all the particulars. She had stopped running. This moment was life enough...When all of a sudden she heard...huffing and puffing....

Woman : AGHHH, Ahh, AGHHH, Ahh, OHHoooo....

EFW: What? I didn't move far enough?

Woman: No, that's not it. Please, you have to understand. My thirteen-year-old son says, "Ma! Maa!! Who do you think you are? How can you kick that poor woman off the beach? She's not doing anything. She's just basically, like, just sitting there…like whatever—upside down and inside out— whatever. Let her stay! Geez." So—you've got to come back. You've got to stay. PLEASE!

EFW: Not so fast….

(Bow/Dancer Pose)

She was not used to being on vacation. She was not used to being interrupted on vacation. Still she had to admit she was a little relieved to be needed.

EFW: Okay. For your 13-year-old, I'll stay.

(Moves everything back.)

Woman: Oh, thank you! I knew you'd understand. I just knew it!
You have my express permission to stay!"

EFW: Right. OK. I guess you think I'm your guest.

(Half Headstand)

She was at peace in all the particulars. She had stopped running.
This moment was life enough.

When all of a sudden she heard: "AHEM!"

And she turned to see the master of the house in his Speedo, the 13-year-old boy by his side.

(Seated Spinal Twist)

The man had a long scar running from the top of his chest to the top of his bathing suit. It glinted in the sun. Heart attack, she wondered?

(Rag Doll)

EFW: It's so lovely of you to let me stay on your private beach.

Man: We'd prefer it if you moved on.

EFW: Hunh??

(Mountain Pose)

Man: We'd prefer it if you moved on. We'd **prefer** it if you moved on!

EFW: You're not kidding. Okay. Right, sure.

(Pack up, moves on.)

She watched the father and son push off from the empty beach in their sailfish.
Was she?
A: A coward?
B: A pacifist?
C: *On va-ca-tion!*

(Moves back to the orginal spot. Tree Pose to Warrior II)

EFW: You know, driving up here I heard a news report about Demi Moore. Apparently, she was filming an underwater nude scene. Nothing unusual in that. The hair floated, the arms and legs danced, but the breasts just sank. She ran screaming from the projection room, called the producer, and demanded a stand-in with real breasts.

EFW: Even Demi Moore?!

(Racing Dive. Sit in beach chair.)

EFW: Maillot, cut-out, jungle print bikini, strapless, braless, net bag, thong!.

(Takes a **'No Trespassing'** *sign from her beach bag. Places it over her chest, reclines.)*

Letter to
LYSISTRATA

LETTER TO LYSISTRATA (2012)

A letter to Lysistrata sent by ephemeral post—backwards in time.

June 9, 2012 AD

Ms. Lysistrata
c/o Aristophanes
Athens, Greece.

Dear Lysistrata,

You said,
Never underestimate the power of a woman.
We're not slaves.
We're free born women and when we're scorned, we're full of fury.
Never underestimate the power of a woman.

Thank you for saying that.
And in 411 BC.
You, imagined by Aristophanes,
You, a fiction, are real to me.

I know, I know,
all women are to some degree or other imagined.
But like I said, you, a fiction, are real to me.

I think you are fucking fabulous
For the simplicity of your attack.
Him, too. Aristophanes.
You and Aristophanes, author and character together
create a comedy about a logically viable solution
to the conundrum of war.

The Trojan War raged for 21 years and in your play you convince wives from

both sides of the conflict to agree to refuse to have sex with their husbands until the men stop fighting and peace is restored. The funny thing is, it works.
It's simple. It's practical.

And in 2012,
I'm sorry to tell you that we've had 8 million 763 thousand 362 days
to make your plan the law of the land.
But violence rages on.

In 2012 AD
wives withholding sex from their husbands to achieve peace is quaint.
F-iiiing, quaint.

Today sex sells anything you can imagine.
A plan of withholding sex as a power play is impossible.

Why, just a year ago one of our illustrious politicians and world leaders packaged pictures of his member in tweets (think little carrier pigeons); another one didn't bother to use Trojans (gloves for the penis) so children were born to his housekeeper (read: slave) and his wife on the same day; another one was accused of raping the maid (read: slave) while she tried to make the bed.
Their wives stood by them. Stood by them.

And this year, one of our warriors stiffed a prostitute in an occupied country where the oldest profession is still legal and offered to pay $28 of an $800 tab. Since at least twelve other soldiers were implicated in similar assignations, our government formed a 'Professionalism Reinforcement Working Group' to assure the public that no state secrets were spilled. Clearly the working group is not investigating labor laws.

And there's more. A former serious contender for President of The United States was accused of using campaign funds to cover up an affair with a pregnant mistress, carried on while the wife lay dying of breast cancer. In court he reportedly flirted with a juror who flirted back. The wife's dead. What happened to the mistress and the baby? The grown daughter, by the wife, stood by him in court. A hung jury.

Lysistrata, I'm not even sure you and Aristophanes could make this stuff up.

In 2012 AD
What if we do try a return to your simple plan and use
sex to stop war?

Imagine an army of virtual prostitutes—holograms of satisfaction.
Sexual drones commanded by geek women and men in Virginia
who make surgical, sexual strikes on perpetrators of war around the globe

HEAVEN ON EARTH
IS LOGICALLY POSSIBLE.

and when that's done, on narcissistic politicians and predatory priests.

A high command unit of flesh and blood prostitutes—well-paid, well-medicated, highly skilled professionals—could easily infiltrate government cabinets, royal palaces and top military sites to make sex/war on these idiots—north and south, east and west—until they are spent and fall fast, fast asleep.

This squadron of sexual seals deserve salaries paid for their services, including bonuses, commensurate with top level lawmakers and CEOs who fucked our particular economy into submission.

This is not sex for power or sex for money. This is sex for STOP!
This is Sex for Peace. This is Sex for Survival. And it creates jobs. Jobs.

And while the bastards sleep, we will recalibrate, rebuild, feed, clothe, heal.

And for the ones who have given up sex because of age or a Viagra disaster, but still thrill to the turn on of waging economic and environmental war on the planet and its inhabitants, imagine a group of Buddhist nuns and priests in tight walking meditation who surround the money warriors, one at a time, and torture them with zazen-sitting meditation, their legs numb and useless until they embrace loving kindness. And when they do, they painfully unfold to see themselves surrounded by well-wishers for their peace and our survival.

It's so very simple.
And not.

Recently I've noticed that two things can be true at once:

war & peace
love & hate
young & old
rich & poor
hungry & full
wet & dry
cold & hot
smart & not smart
free & enslaved
noble & not
tragic & comic

Do you know that peace is still defined by reference to war?
Peace is the absence of war.
War is defined as itself.
Conflict is our primary condition.

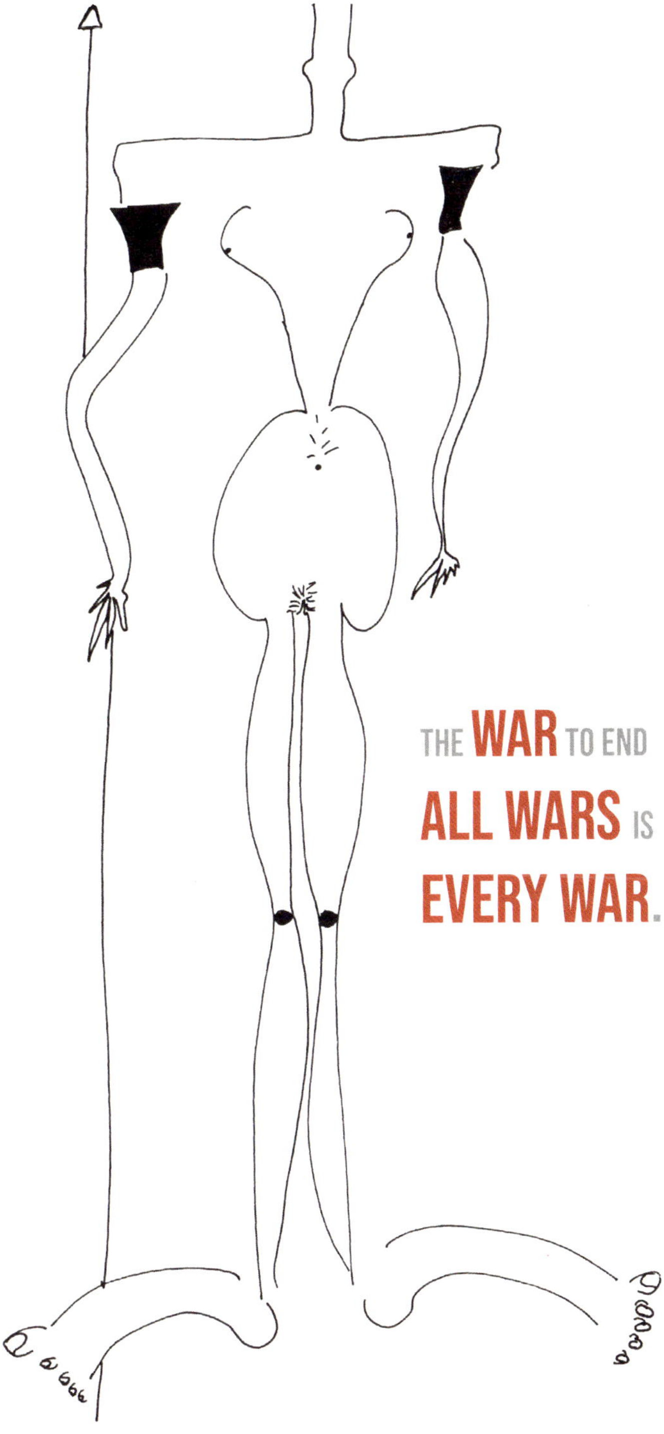

THE **WAR** TO END **ALL WARS** IS **EVERY WAR**.

Peace as the absence of war? Really?
This is a testosterone-driven definition.

To the men I love. (You know who you are.)
This is not personal. It's not about you.
It is the result of centuries of hormonally driven definitions.
What would an estrogen-infused definition of war be?
A very simple reversal: War is the absence of peace.

Let's make peace the reference point, the new normal.
Peace is our default setting.
War is the aberration.
To achieve this,
We need a fierce peace.
Peace as a fierce and full serenity of living and loving,
as in heaven on earth.

To be sustainable, peace must be erect, energetic.

How else to defeat the drama of war?
(And climate change. It's bigger than war.)
Ah-ha! In the time we have left, we
defeat the drama of war through sports,
art & music, theater & dance
(shameless plug for arts education)

(Dance break)

We will be saved by games
that offer us the spectacle of a pretend life and death struggle,
where there is no actual loss of life or collateral damage to bystanders.
It will be a fierce and frothy peace.

Think: The Celtics vs Miami.
Or the battle to defy gravity in a new production of *Swan Lake.*
By the way, we're all in a life and death struggle
against gravity, right?
Why can't that be enough of a battle?

The war to end all wars is every war.
We come to our bloody senses and before long fight again.
Are we captured by the rapture of amnesia
or simply by a failure of the imagination?

Lysistrata, we give prizes for peace. But get this: Alfred Nobel, who founded the
Nobel Peace Prize, was the inventor of dynamite.

Aristophanes might have edited this out as too improbable.

And there's more. In 1896, a French newspaper erroneously printed
Alfred's obituary rather than that of his brother, Ludvig,
who exploited oil fields along the Caspian Sea.
It read: *Alfred Nobel who became rich by finding ways*
to kill more people faster than ever before died yesterday.

Clearly, Nobel wanted his legacy to be more estrogen-driven.
So unbeknownst to his family,
he left money posthumously for the award
that honors the reduction of standing armies
and the promotion of peace congresses.
In his way, he joined your army, Lysistrata.

You'll be glad to know that some of us in the 21st century do listen to you. In 2011, just before it was too late to work, Leymah Gbowee, a warrior for peace, won a Nobel Prize for instigating a sex strike of women on both sides of the civil war in Liberia. Peace came.

Dear Lysistrata:
Thank you for reminding us that
heaven on earth is logically possible.

It's tragic and comic that 8 million 763 thousand 362 days after your plan
we still ravage the world with the conundrum of war.

An erect peace could be our primary condition.

Love to you always,
Ara

PS. And primary peace & serenity to Aristophanes, too!

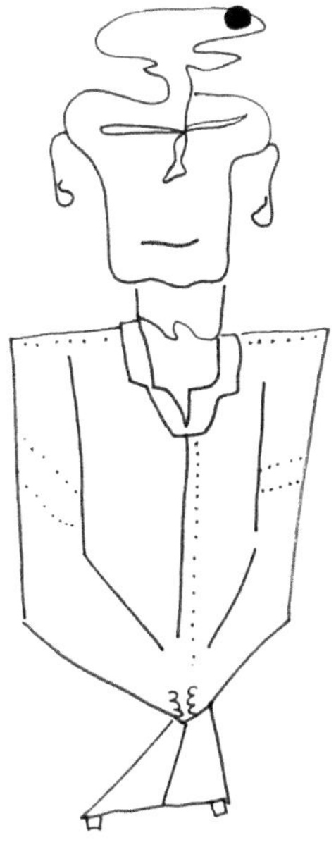

THIS IS
DEPRESSING.
LET'S
PRETEND
IT'S
NOT
HAPPENING.

Why Did Sarah Bernhardt Sleep in a Coffin?

WHY DID SARAH BERNHARDT SLEEP IN A COFFIN? (2018)

The present instantly becomes the future
and so is simultaneously the past.
The present instantly becomes the future
and so is simultaneously the past.
The present instantly becomes the future
and so is simultaneously the past.
The present instantly becomes the future
and so is simultaneously the past.

It's a continuum after all.

To be or not to be?
To see or not to see?
To flee or not to flee?
Oh, right. It's just
To be or not to be?
That is the question.

It is said that the great 19th-century actress Sarah Bernhardt
slept in a coffin.

A quote from her comes down to us through time.
Perhaps it is true.
She says, "My bedroom was very tiny. The big bamboo bed took up all the room.
In front of the window was my coffin, where I frequently installed myself
to learn my lines."

To be or not to be?
To see or not to see?
To flee or not to flee?
Oh, right. It's just to be or not to be.

Why did the legendary Sarah Bernhardt, queen of the stage,
study her lines in a coffin?

Slight shadows emerge
Breathless from the heart.
Only of death can we be certain.

Did the divine Sarah Bernhardt nap?
Did she nap in a coffin?
Well, how do you want to spend your time?
Awake or asleep?
How do you want to spend your life?

Spend has end embedded in it.
Death is a noun ground into dust.

This is depressing.
Let's pretend it's not happening.

When my younger sister died at fifty
leaving behind her husband and sons, fifteen and eleven,
our aunt, then in her eighties, said quietly,
"It has to be OK."
I felt a moment of rage, like a Christian slap.
It's not OK. It's not OK. It's not OK!
Then a curious comfort,
surrender to the loss of every beloved one and ourselves.

Yes. I am pretending to be on a crowded New York City subway
grateful to have a spot to hang on.
On this rush hour train,
I think, "Oh, right, everyone in this car will die.
We get off at different stops, but we all ride the D train."

My mother's ashes are in a small box.
She died in 2001.

My mother had a melodious voice and was kind beyond measure.
A childhood friend said to me,
"You think I'm coming to play with you
but I'm really coming over to see your mother."
I understood my good fortune and learned early to share.
We who loved her were bitter with her loss and sang praises in memoriam.

Yes, my mother's ashes are in a small box.
She died in 2001.
Ashes have a way of slipping to the back of the closet.

In my anguish for not having figured out

where the dust of my mother wanted to travel,
my beloved partner reminds me how much she loved
New York City and so enjoys being here with us.

My partner's beloved mother's ashes are in a small box.
She died in 2011.
She spoke with a strong Austrian accent.
In 1938, as a teenager in Vienna,
she had the courage. To see. That she had to flee.
On the last train out. In order to be.

In eternity, it is never too late to celebrate our loved ones
who quietly watch and wait.
They know. Or there is no knowing.

Why did Sarah Bernhardt sleep in a coffin?
Perhaps she created a little play about death
and during the run of her show,
if she awoke in her coffin, she bounded on stage
in present tense surprise and delight,
never for a moment really believing she would die.

The present instantly becomes the future
and so is simultaneously the past.
The present instantly becomes the future
and so is simultaneously the past.
The present instantly becomes the future
and so is simultaneously the past.

It's a continuum after all.

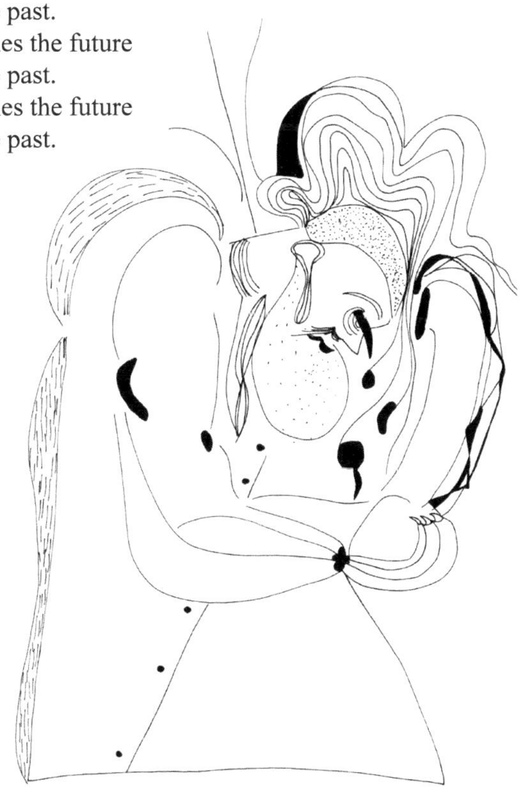

Setting A Place For Carl

SETTING A PLACE FOR CARL (2013)

A Place:

A cloth. A plate. A knife. A fork. A spoon. A cup.
Pouring life....

Are you like me?

Every time I see *Romeo and Juliet* I want to rush the stage and scream, "No! Romeo! Don't do it. Don't drink the poison. She's alive! Can't you see the roses in her cheeks? Oh, Romeo. Not so fast. Slow down, Romeo!"

But once he has killed himself and Juliet decides to take her own life, I understand, "Oh, yes, go ahead— kill yourself, Juliet. How can your love be dead? How could this have happened? What can you live for now that your love is gone?"

What if Romeo and Juliet survived?

They did, you know.

Muse on the following:
Friar Lawrence has no shortage of access to potions, polemics, and magic. In a surprise plot twist, the mishap with the letter is undone by the good Friar who cooks up an antidote to the actual poison Romeo took so when Juliet awakes she is able to set right to work nursing her Romeo, who rather too much enjoys the attention.
Puck makes a surprise appearance from *A Midsummer Night's Dream* and pours an untested elixir in Romeo's ear. Romeo stops groaning and has a speedy recovery. Juliet gets her Romeo back. Puck gets it right for once.

And the good Friar reminds the young couple:

Friar: *These violent delights have violent ends*
And in their triumph die, like fire and powder,
Which as they kiss consume. The sweetest honey

Is loathsome in his own deliciousness
And in the taste confounds the appetite.
Therefore love moderately: long love doth so:
Too swift arrives too tardy as too slow.

Romeo and Juliet are alive! All's well that ends well, except that Romeo and Juliet know that despite triumphing over mishaps and stabbings and poisonings in pursuit of proving that they cannot live without each other, there remain a few troubling issues to consider:

1. The shock of their deaths is the only thing that has brought peace to their warring families.

2. In two weeks, or as soon as they get used to the idea that their beloved children have survived, each family will get to work to tear them apart.

3. Romeo will be jailed, hanged, or exiled. The feud will resume.

4. Their marriage will be annulled and Juliet doomed to an unhappy union of convenience to Paris who is waiting in the wings.

5. Even if Romeo is pardoned, gets out of the murder rap, and both families forgive them, there is still a problem. There is no more *Romeo and Juliet*—the play.

6. The young lovers will be resigned to 'happily ever after.' Have you ever read a sequel that follows 'happily ever after?' As it turns out, a contented couple is interesting only to the couple.

8. R & J are young and impetuous but not stupid. They have observed their parents. And though they thought they would be different, they have heard over and over and over again that passion fades, at which point there is a lot of kissing 'by the book,' if even that. They'd rather die than endure 'kissing by the book.'

9. They are doomed. They are alive but they are doomed, already yearning for young love, weeping for lost love. They decide to preserve the play.

10. They are buried alive/dead and revived by the faithful Friar. They escape and hide out in Mantua or Arden, their heaven on earth. They vow to keep their escape secret.

The secret keeps their love alive.
Oh, Romeo and Juliet.

I think of my friend Elaine and a story told at her memorial.
She loved her Carl. He died too young and unexpectedly from a medical mishap. Ever after Carl's death, and especially in restaurants, Elaine set a place at the table for him. And now they are both gone.

In remembrance, young love lives forever.

A Place:

A cloth. A plate. A fork. A knife. A spoon. A cup.
Pouring life….

Act II scene ii

(Carl as Romeo)
Romeo: *But soft, what light through yonder window breaks?*
It is the East and Juliet is the sun!

(Elaine as Juliet)
Juliet: *O Romeo, Romeo! Wherefore art thou Romeo?*

Juliet: *My bounty is as boundless as the sea,*
My love as deep; the more I give to thee,
The more I have for both are infinite.

Act III, scene ii
Juliet: *Come night; come Romeo; come thou day in night;*
For thou wilt lie upon the wings of night
Whiter than new snow upon a raven's back.
Come gentle night; come loving, black browed night;
Give me my Romeo; and when he shall die,
Take him and cut him out in little stars,
And he will make the face of heaven so fine
That all the world will be in love with night
And pay no worship to the garish sun.

Romeo: *I would I were thy bird.*

Juliet: *Sweet, so would I*
Yet I would kill thee with much cherishing
Good night, good night
Parting is such sweet sorrow….

ONE HAS TO AGE. ONE AGES;
WHAT A **SURPRISE!**
IN OLD AGE, ONE HAS MORE
STORIES TO TELL.

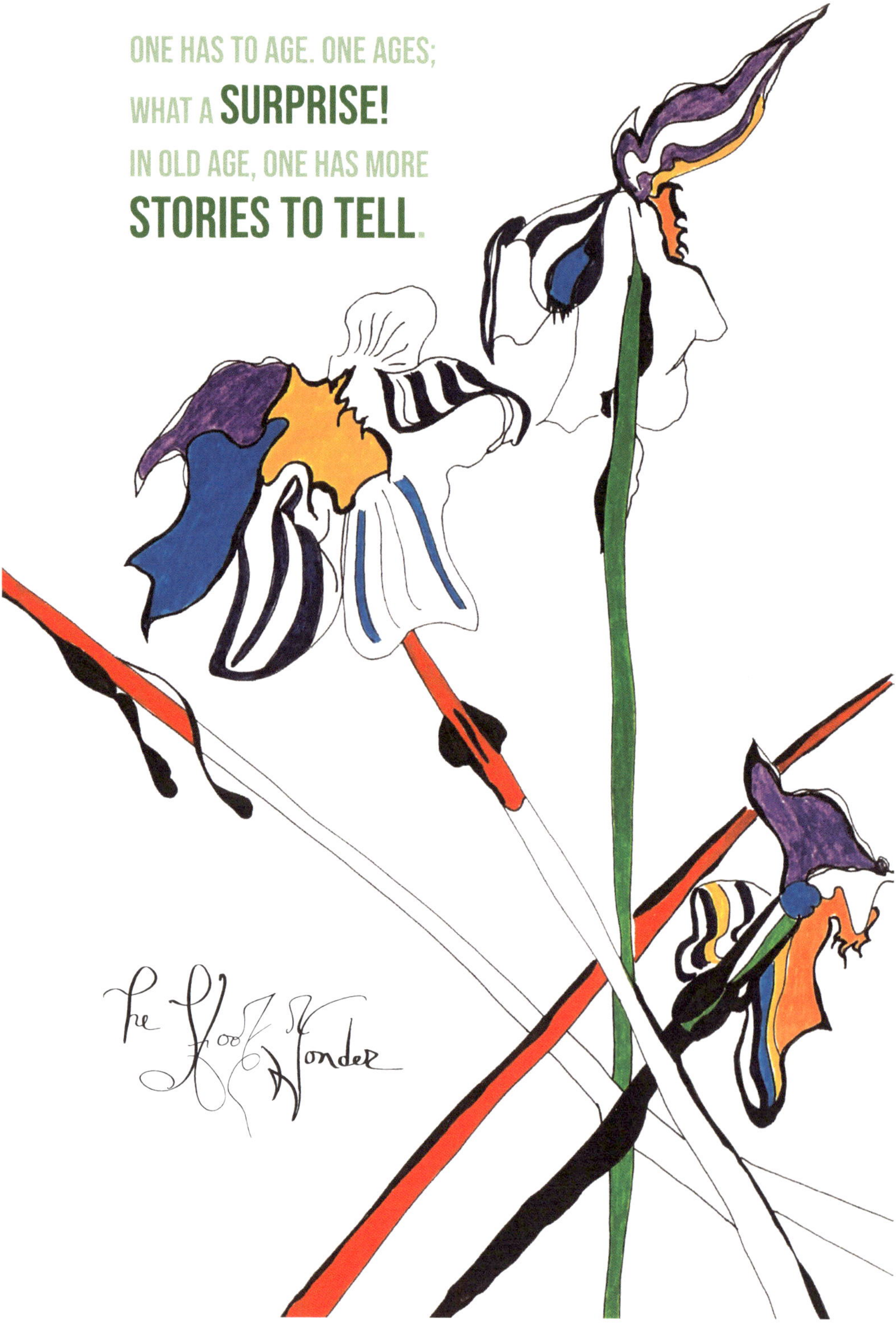

THE HOOK OF WONDER (2014)

Wendy, Wendy, when you are sleeping in your silly bed
you might be flying about with me
saying funny things to the stars.

So said Peter Pan to Wendy in the fairy tale by J.M. Barrie.

In a real-life story, old, I mean elder, Wendy is dating an elder Peter Pan—
not the fictional Pan— but a living, aging person
who refuses to give up his sense of wonder.

He regales her with quotes from the fairy tale
as he climbs in her window.
And out again— of course.

Sometimes, now that they are old,
Wendy forgets to open the window.
Here he comes
singing, 'Cock-A-Doodle-Do!'
Crash! Ouch!

Wendy reminds herself to hold the handrail
as she goes down the steps to the backyard
where Peter lies crumpled from his fall.

Wendy builds a little house around him
and plays his nurse/wife/mother.
Healing occurs and off he wanders.

She returns to her knitting.
Oh my, he's back already.
Remember the window!

Good one!

Peter lands smoothly on the windowsill,
unfurls a tattered map,
points to the spot of their next great adventure,
risks a deep knee bow to her,
loses his balance on the narrow sill,
teeters, bumps into the sash, slips off the lintel,
and lands once more on his back in the backyard.

Wendy remembers to hold the railing
as she hurries to the yard.

She arrives just in time to watch the tattered map,
float gently down,
alighting on his face like a paper tent,
a little pointed hat or his shadow.

Peter assures her he's just fine.
He sits up slowly. She slowly sits down.
They discuss the details of their next escapade,
despite the complexity about to ensue
as they attempt to help each other stand up.

Their adventures come with no repeats;
not a single place or rose or idea is ever the same.
They have been to hundreds of out-of-the way places—
caves, countries, tops of trees, tents by the sea, beds made of moss.

They see movies in the stars, histories in rocks,
sweet sadness in seashells, and joy in every gentle breeze.

Peter and Wendy have had tea with Indian princesses,
drinks with pirates, oatmeal with lost boys,
and more than once been happily lost in the woods.

Permanence of home, of love, of life
remain more curious illusions
than anything in Wonderland.
Brave of heart, Peter Pan the Elder
is wise to the idea of permanence.

Peter Pan the Younger— Pan of the fairy tale—
is trapped in timelessness.

That little pint-sized oppositional narcissist
who we all love to love will never age.
He won't grow up!

None of us want to. But he won’t.

Young Pan can’t even remember his own story,
is terrible at telling tall tales to entertain his lost boys,
and needs a Wendy to feed, clothe, and read to them.

When Wendy begins to age,
Peter tries to woo her to stay in Neverland.
He declares, *One girl is worth more than 20 boys.*

Wendy startles at this pickup line
that hints at free food and servitude
and makes her exit back into time.
Peter feels abandoned, and resumes the dating game.
He repeats the same speed date with Wendy’s daughter, Jane,
and then her granddaughter, Margaret,
and on and on over the generations,
swiping right— or is it left?
Straight on til morning.

Peter Pan of the fairy tale chooses to live frozen in time
where growing up is a dead issue.

Is the ageless young Peter already dead?
Why is age the big dread?

Perhaps it is he who escorts children
who have died to heaven,
like an EMT of the afterlife.

Elder Wendy quotes from J.M. Barrie,
We came from the seed
of those babies whose first laugh birthed a fairy.
Who fell out of our perambulators
and became lost boys and girls.

In and out of Elder Wendy's window
an aging, courageous, Elder Peter climbs,
reminding Wendy that Young Fictional Peter
was right when he said,
I suppose it's like the ticking crocodile, isn't it?
Time is chasing after all of us.

Wendy wonders, then why am I sitting here
in this old house knitting?
Why do I busy myself with this and that obligation?

I shall fly away, whenever I can.
Wish-winged. Half-winged. Partially dusted....
Second to the right and straight on till morning.

I'll play Peter Pan!
Like Maude Allen, Cathy Rigby, Sandy Duncan, and Mary Martin.

What a marvel or a disaster
that for decades actresses, grown women,
have flown overhead as this little rapscallion.

She realizes that the two syndromes,
The Peter Pan Syndrome—
people who refuse to grow up and take responsibility—
and the Wendy Syndrome—
people devoted to a life of servitude and happily ever after—
are both delusional.

She thinks, "Oh, Wendy, even sitting still,
you can fly in your imagination.
Open your palms. Let the breeze through."

To stay in Neverland,
one must never land.
Life in Never Neverland
is a perpetual adventure with no surprises.

One has to age.
One ages; what a surprise!

In old age, one has more stories to tell.
What a surprise!
Together we face the ticking Croc
and know love without condition
in the face of loss.
Such is the hook of wonder.

Oh! Here comes Elder Peter Pan
crowing and quoting J.M. Barrie,

Wendy, Wendy, when you are sleeping in your silly bed
you might be flying about with me
saying funny things to the stars.

Odd things happen to all of us
on our way through life
without our noticing.

Wendy, would you like an adventure now,
or would you like to have your tea first?

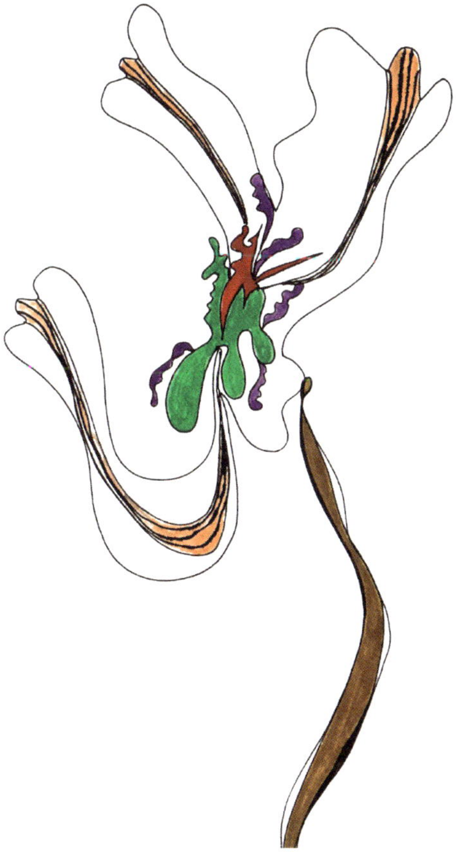

Off Her Rocker

OFF HER ROCKER (2021)

(Sitting in a rocking chair. Hands folded in lap, not rocking.)

> *Repose is a quality too many undervalue. In the clamor, one is irresistibly drawn to the woman who sits gracefully relaxed, who keeps her hands still, talks in a low voice and listens with responsive eyes, and smiles. She creates a spell around her, charming to the ear, eye and mind.*
>
> Good Housekeeping Magazine, 1947.

1947— the year I was born. *Good Housekeeping* gives me a glimpse of what my mother was up against. Young women, elegantly silenced in the service of peace, make a place of honor for their men recently returned from World War II.

My mother was born in 1919.
In the United States women won the right to vote in 1920.
Please don't forget this.

When I was eight years old, my mother told me a story her mother told her, of women in Victorian England whose babies were placed on wooden boards and set on their laps. The young mothers could look but were instructed not to touch their infants. If the baby cooed, smiled, rolled over, whimpered, or wailed, the mother was not to touch the baby.

This was to teach what?
Please don't forget this question.

Fortunately, my mother and her mother were defiant huggers.

Everything comes from the Mother Tree.

And so we begin.

(Begin rocking)

A young mother rocks a baby.
Alone, an elder rocks an elder.
Beings in time.

Begin with the ordinary, the common-place
The necessity of back and forth.
Effortlessly repeated.

A young mother rocks a baby
An elder rocks an elder.
Endlessly shared.
Endlessly repeated.

As a little girl, I thought I would
just rock and roll through life.
I hopped off my mother's lap
and twirled into childhood dreams of the ballet.

(Stop rocking. Tour jeté hand dance.)

I just did seven tour jetés and landed in a perfect arabesque.
Did you see it?

Things I no longer do
that I never did:

> Downhill skiing: see ballet.
> Jockey in the Kentucky Derby: too heavy by age 12.
> Dancer with Alvin Ailey: crooked elbows.
> Tree Surgeon: see jockey.
> Heart Surgeon: see dreams.

Arctic explorer: the ice is melting.
Mathematician: they peak at 28.
Head Stand: see the Yoga of good intentions.

(Begin rocking)

Rock and roll. Rock and roll.
Bend your knees and roll up.

(Off the rocking chair to stand)

Tree pose!

Turns out, it is the intention to be a tree that counts.
Feel the roots spreading out though the feet.
Tiny foot bones like roots at the end of the tree trunk of a leg.

I know, it's a cliché. I'm a cliché.
What about you?

A little music, please. Ah, yes….

(Dance of Trees)

The spine rises as an elderberry tree,
And finds an old growth forest in the joints.
Here's a pine spine— prickly—
or an even older, ever stronger oak,
or the jolly beech tree,
whose brown paper leaves flutter right on through winter.

The rings around an elder's spine recall the bend of the sapling.
Wrinkles like the rings of a tree at the throat, the elbow, and the knee.
We become one with the Mother Tree.

(Return to chair. Begin rocking.)

Come to think of it,
this rocker is made of a tree.
Branches of the Mother Tree.

A walking stick is made of a tree.
A wooden leg is made of a tree.
A house is made of trees.
Bowls and boards can be made of trees.
A bentwood chair—wood from a tree.

(The rocking gets bumpy. Ear close to the chair, listening.)

The rocking chair has a story to share,
says it's about a bentwood friend.
The chair is addressing its owner.
The chair speaks,
"You put me outside.
But I'm an inside chair.
I see you looking out at me,
right through that dirty picture window.
Admiring your work, putting me in the yard—
or was that out to pasture?"

"I am not a cow. I am a chair.
Here I sit planted in the backyard with nothing to do.
Stationary. Well, of course, stationary, I am a chair.
I used to hold people. They loved sitting on me.
I offered a welcome spot to rest and served happily.
So why was I taken to the yard?"

"Is it because the caning on my seat is broken?
I am sorry you can no longer sit on me."

"Come to think of it,
I wasn't broken before you sat down.
And now I need to be caned!
Not beaten. Restrung."

"You, who thought you owned me, were the last person to sit on me.
Now I'm a broken chair shoved behind the house.
But at heart I am still a delicate chair. A delicate flower."

"Flowers!
I heard you announce that you will put a thick wooden board
over my unhinged woven seat so you can put a flowering plant there."

"Why not a person?"

"You think I'd make a nice planter; I'd make a nice planter, you think.
What kind of an idea is this? How exactly is this going to work?"

"Adaptive reuse of me who used to be a favored chair?
I am not some paper clip with an accompanying piece of string
used to demonstrate your creative imagination.
I am a chair. An indoor chair. I am not an outdoor chair."

IT'S THE INTENTION TO **BE** A **TREE** THAT COUNTS

"I know, my caning is so frayed
that a houseguest could fall through the hole
in what might have otherwise been a safe seat—in the house.
Would it be funny if a guest tumbled though the seat and it happened in the yard?"

"An adult butt can plop down on a boarded-over seat no problem.
A grown person can sit on a board,
And I'd be a contributing chair again.
Indoors —at the dining table or in the nursery."
"I have nothing against plants, I love them."

"Especially, trees.
I am a chair. I am a bentwood chair.
I have a heritage.
My mother was a tree.
Hey, it's cold out here."

(The voice of the chair fades away.)

As I was saying before being interrupted by a chair.

Paper is made from trees.
So you're old on paper?
Well, it's about time.

Pencils are made from trees.
A poet puts pencil of tree to paper of tree,
carving the space of the page with swoops and hollows.
Even poems are made of trees.

My mother's penmanship was a near perfection
with her practice of the Palmer method.

Gracious, spacious, elegant cursive loops precisely balanced
and written with efficiency to match the speed of a typewriter.

In a vicious divorce she lost her children who she saw only on weekends. She was alone and destitute. Shamed and not released into some entrepreneurial freedom, she secured a job as a travel agent. An ardent team player, underpaid, she lived above the agency in a tiny apartment and overworked. She would go downstairs to the office at any time of night to finish a ticket or clean up a mess. Tickets in these days were handwritten.

Hers were a thing of beauty.
At times I thought this a colossal waste of her time.
Why write such elegant script on an airline ticket?

Wealthy clients might not even notice.
For poorer clients, it was a kind of loving attention she could offer.

Years later, I realized how essential this artistic indulgence was.
It was an act of control, of doing more than was asked, of presenting perfection
by a woman who had been emotionally and economically cast adrift.

Another detour in the woods.
Crazy thought…what about men and trees?
And not the clear-cutting kind. The poetic ones.
Who, even if not known, have not been forgotten.

I never met my grandfather, Elwood Tabor.
He died when my mother was 19.
Elwood. Elwood, Wood—
I notice that his name includes
a reference to the wood of trees.

My grandfather's college roommate was Joyce Kilmer.
I never met Joyce Kilmer.

In 1913 Kilmer wrote the poem *Trees.*
Memorized by generations of school children,
minimized as a cliché by generations of poets,
memorialized in a rest stop named after him
on the New Jersey Turnpike.

Begin with the ordinary, the common-place,
the necessity of back and forth, back and forth,
endlessly repeated.

In joy, in love, boundaries disappear.

Wrinkles like the rings of a tree at the elbows and knees.
Everything comes back to the Mother Tree.

Coming to the end of dancing.
There's no end to dancing.

Please remember this.

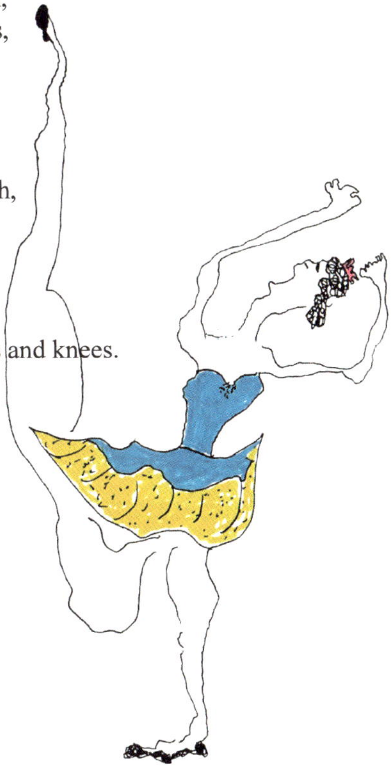

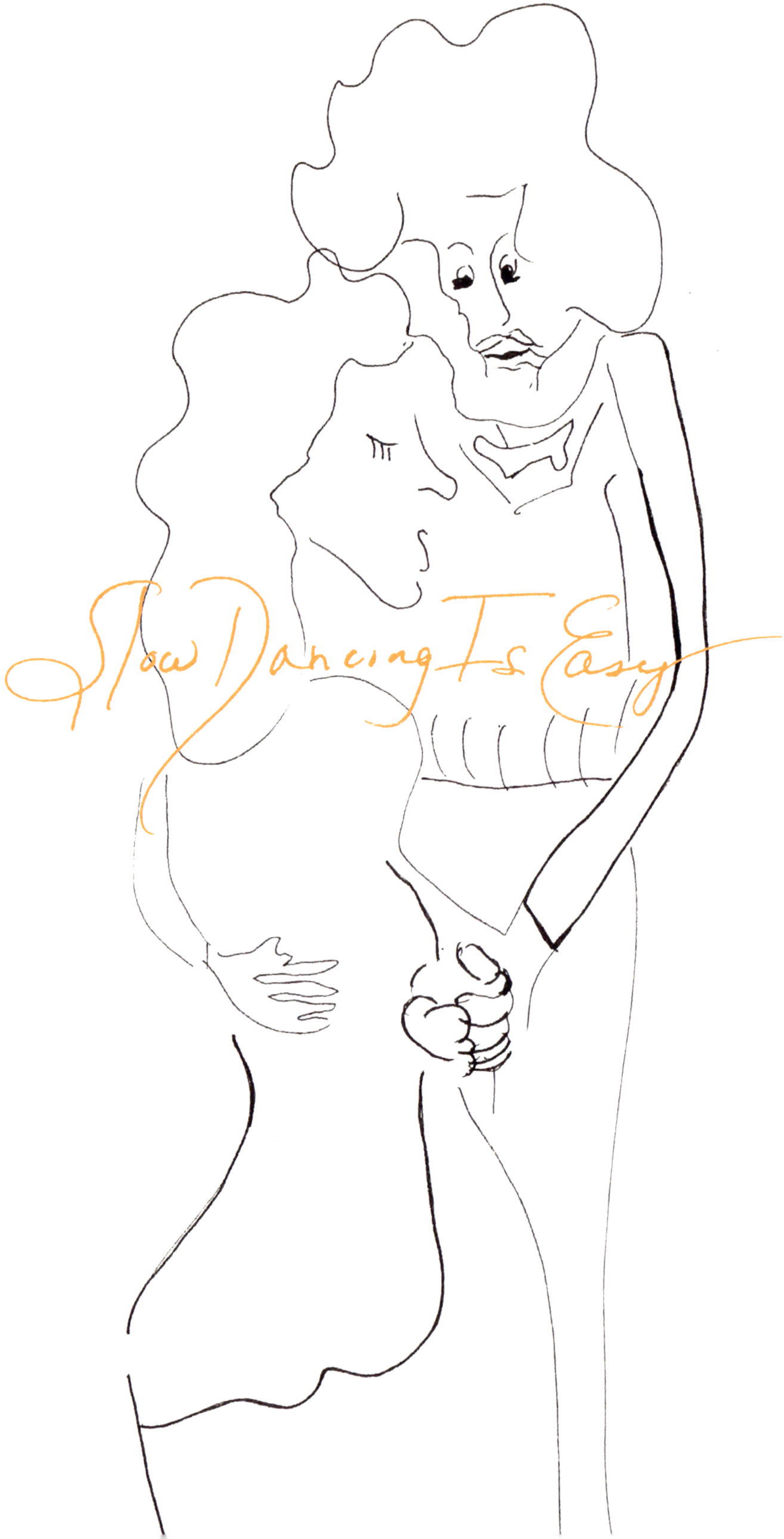
Slow Dancing Is Easy

SLOW DANCING IS EASY (2010)

Slow dancing is easy.
Why should it be hard?

Slow dancing is easy because
it's almost always only about the hold.
That rooted shuffle in the feet
exists purely as a justification for hanging on so tight.
It's an upper body event
built upon the reality of two left feet.

I didn't say it wasn't complex.

Take, for instance, two fourteen-year-old hearts
about to burst
whose owners nestle
in the curved nest of shoulder and neck,
or who simply contemplate—an ear.

Who can be surprised
by a strand of hair.
His hair in her eye — ticklish, painful, welcome.
Or volumes of her curls,
like an oxygen mask at his face.

If both happen to turn their heads at the same moment—
the lips are surprisingly close.
Who thought of this slow dancing thing?

Why there's:
The Foxtrot
The Foxtrot

The Bunny Hop
The Foxtrot
The Bunny Hop
The Turkey Trot
The Monkey
The Chicken
The Jitterbug

And the Samba, the Salsa, and the Meringue!

And the Waltz, Viennese and American

And the Tango!

Finally, the Tango!

Left foot: Slow
Right Foot: Slow
Left foot, right foot: quick, quick.
Slow.

Try that again:
Slow, slow,
Quick, quick, quick, quick
Slow.

Try that again.
And end with

Steam, swivel, flick, dip!

These dances are hard.
Hard enough to make
Arthur Murray a millionaire
and Fred Astaire a god.

Don't forget the Cha-cha.
The cha, cha, cha, cha, cha.
A traveling dance.
A dance of cha-change.

Sweet turn and straight ahead—
has anybody seen my partner?
Or my shoes?

OK.
Going on, with imaginary friends.
Who never get lost or step on our feet.

In the middle years, slow dancing is easy
because it can happen
for a minute in your car
but only at stoplights,
in your cubicle at work,
and back home
in the kitchen with the radio on,
between chop and boil and scrub the tub.

"Oh, Hi!
How was your day?"
You don't say.
"It's your turn to give the baby a bath.
Where are you disappearing to in such a hurry?
You live here. "

"Lost your sense of humor, sweetie?
Me too.
Care to join me in my kinesphere?"

"Hang on tight.
We can slow dance all night.
or for a minute
before the baby wails."

Rest him on your shoulder and rock
left foot, right foot, left foot, right foot.
It's the slow spin lullaby.

And then the later years suddenly waltz by.

And in the later, later years,
slow dancing is still easy.
But as you can see,
finding a partner and your shoes can be hard.

"Care to join me in a movable hug?"

I said,

"Care

to join me

in a movable hug?"

Remember the limbo?
That was about how low can you go.

This one's about how slow can you go.

"Come this way, over here. You can do it.
Just for a minute.
Bring your walker over here."

Slow dancing!
Calms the heart rate or increases it
depending on age.

Slow dancing is easy because you can do it
when the floodwaters rise
and humming is all that's left.
The final partner,
invisible as air.

Slow dancing can turn a minute into a minuet.
Hold onto each other tight.
Make that minute minuet last.

Indefinite,

indeterminate,

indescribable,

obstinate.

Infinite.

ON LOOKING BACK (2006)

Over and over and over again —every time the story is told—
I still step on that damn snake.
Oops!

Some of you may recall the story of Orpheus and Eurydice
But in case you don't, here's a little refresher:
Orpheus and Eurydice.
Eurydice and Orpheus.

Of all mortals, Orpheus made the most beautiful music.
She was his beloved. His "Euuurydicccee."

In joyous celebration of their marriage, she cavorted in a field.
Silly girl.
She stepped on a snake.
She died.

Orpheus bemoaned his fate,
the sudden loss of his wife,
with such grace of song that the gods wept.

Sisyphus stopped pushing his rock, among other things.

Orpheus could not live without his beloved
so he traveled to the underworld to beg the gods
to restore the thread of life to his Eurydice.
He would prove love stronger than death!
Silly man.

The gods granted his request.
Orpheus could guide his Eurydice back to the land of the living.

Footnote: There was just one simple condition.
During the journey, he must not look back.

Footnote: Virgil
At the very point not far below the verge of upper earth,
Orpheus, fearing lest Eurydice should fall,
and impatient to behold her once again,
turned his eyes and at once she sank back again.
Hapless woman stretching out her hands
and struggling for the arms of her lover,
she caught nothing but empty air.

Dying a second time,
she complained not of her husband,
for why she should complain of being so beloved?

ORPHEUS!

Footnote: Anonymous

What were you thinking?
Or were you not thinking?
Have you no faith?
Have you no faith in me?
Or is it that you just can't follow directions?

I mean, consider me before you look back.
Consult me. You never consult me.
You don't even ask me if I want to follow you back.
You just assume.
And then against the gods you look back
and send me back a fool.

ORPEHUS LOOK AT ME!
You can look at me *now.*

Do you really think all I want to do is come back
to wash your socks, polish your strings, and listen while you sing?
Give me a little credit!
I may not be billable,
but I'm half the song.

The gods trick you.
They know you and they trick you.
Yes, they weep with your loss,
but they're the producers.
You're just the talent.
It's not always about you!

How long exactly do you think they'll let Sisyphus stop pushing that bloody rock?
Among other things.
Hunh? How long?

And what if I come back and you die?
What then?
I'm as good as dead, again, again.

Why so thoughtless, my love?
Footnote: Virgil
Then she pronounced that last farewell which he scarcely heard,
and again, she was hurried back from whence she had come.
And Orpheus was astounded and perplexed
by this two-fold loss of his wife.

Oh, Orpheus.
How I wish you could hear me.
So many songs and sonnets, poems and plays
are written about us. And in some of them,
I'm even mentioned by name.

Oops!
Over and over and over again. Every time the story is told,
I still step on that damn snake.

THE UNDERPINNING OF **MAGIC** IS **TRUTH**

PART II

THE GHOST OF P. T. BARNUM SPEAKS

Watch the Bullies Dance

WATCH THE BULLIES DANCE (2017)

The Ghost of P.T. Barnum, upset that heaven is a no-smoking zone and enraged that he has been compared to our 45th POTUS, emerges back on earth to defend his name and ethics in the showbusiness of politics.

Come One, Come All!

Oh New York City!
It is such pleasure to be here with you where on a good day,
the Golden Rule, the Four Noble Truths,
the Ten Commandments, and the Rule of Law still hold sway
and where we bless Mother Earth
and the Lenape People for the land on which we stand.

Watch carefully while I, the Ghost of P.T. Barnum,
19th- century American circus impresario extraordinaire
and most famous person in the world,
emerge from a puff of my own cigar smoke!

Tada!

A Hoax? A Humbug?

In truth, it is heaven on earth to be back here with you.
Turns out actual heaven is a no-smoking zone.
Close to paradise, but no cigar.
Cigar smoke in, cigar smoke out.
You might call this breathing meditation.
I call it peace.

Ah, just to feel that whip in my hand.

More than 100 years after my death,
I'm still the greatest showman in the world!
And I'm back on Earth to clear my name!

Come one, come all to the United States of America,
The Greatest Show on Earth!
See death-defying acts and freaks of nature!
See your wildest dreams come true!
America, the…

May I have your attention, pleasssssse!

I'm very sorry to have to announce this,
but the big top is full.
It is sold out! America is sold out!
So—
If you don't have a ticket already,
if you don't have a ticket already,
if you don't have a ticket already,
you can just 'fuhgetttabout' it!

Sold America!
Sold Out! Sold Out!
Sold America!
Sold out! Sold out!
Sold America!

Tada!

The Foxy Emperor Of Humbugs

Time for a little fireside chat.

Once upon a time,
I, P.T. Barnum,
entertainer bizarre, king of circuses,
was the most famous person in the world.

I invented fake news!
And sideshows suitable for the whole family.

I was celebrated as the Prince of Humbugs.
That was me!

What's a humbug?
Why, it's just pretending.
It's a hoax, a lie, a magic show
made just for you!
Humbugs?
I like to think of them as 'creative truth.'
Humbugs filled my tents
with happy paying customers!

Back in my day we were all in on the game.
But now America has taken the idea of the circus
all the way to the White House!

(Addressing an imagined POTUS)
Oh, 45….
You did it! You really did it!
You fooled enough of the people, enough of the time.
You and I both know that the more times a lie is repeated,
the more it is costumed as truth.

Oh, no!
Really, I'm just saying, 'WOW!'
I bow wow,
I bow wow,
I bow wow wow down to you—
our chosen one,
our Foxy Emperor of Humbugs!

Yes, sir!
Yes, sir!

Reading is so over.
Science is so over.
Elite affectations!
Reading and Science
No fun!
Leave the academic stuff to the Chinese!
The seas are not rising.
The children are not starving.
A tweet here,
A twat there.
No harm done!
Everything will work out,
now that you are boss.
Yes, sir!
Yes, sir!
No doubt about it, sir!
There is only one truth
and that is: Whatever you say goes!
Yes, yes, of course!
You are the biggest cock….
Oh, no!
I mean, ah…
you are richer than a Koch Brother!

How's the story of *The Emperor's New Clothes*
working for you these days, hunh?
Oh, you didn't read it.

Bah, Humbugs….

Spectacular Press!

Among my many obituaries, here's one from April 8, 1891
that calls my death,
the removal of a noteworthy and almost classical figure,
typical of the age of transparent puffing
through which the modern democracies are passing.
His name is a proverb already,
and will continue to be a proverb
until mankind has ceased to find pleasure
in the comedy of a harmless deceiver
and the willingly deceived.

Monster that I was,
over a hundred years later, I still get spectacular press!
Even today, there are new books, articles, Broadway shows about me.
In the movies, Hugh the Jackman sings and dances as my better self.
And the press even compared me, P.T. Barnum,
to the President of the United States!

How dare they?!
Not 45!

(To an imagined POTUS:)

"You? Really? 16, OK, but you, 45?"

"Yes, I know, we both embraced
the freedom of fabrication to make and lose fortunes.
And rebuild after fires.
But unlike you, I had principles!
Everybody was scared, stupefied but safe under my tent.
Nobody got intentionally hurt.
Nobody threw a real punch."

"You think the audience is stupid.
I never said the audience was stupid.
Blind, but not stupid!
You think you can just send in a fresh set of clowns
to close your deals.
But think about it.
If you lie to inflame a crowd,
they become a mob,
a mob your clowns no longer can control."

“Governing is not showbiz. It’s real life!”

More Spectacular Press!
Headline: *May 17, 1884!*
Jumbo Crosses Bridge. Quells Terror.
The public is stupefied by the newly suspended high wire Brooklyn Bridge.
They are so terrified they refuse to cross.

TRUST NOT FEAR
THAT IS THE ART OF THE SHOWMAN!

So I have my Jumbo, the biggest elephant in the world,
lead the charge of 21 elephants and 17 camels
across the brand-new Brooklyn Bridge.

And why this high wire act?
To scare people?
No!
To prove to the terrified public that the newly suspended Brooklyn Bridge is safe.

TRUST not FEAR. That is the art of the showman!

"You, our dear 45th President,
have taught us that in 1884,
you would have tripled the number of elephants and camels
crossing the Brooklyn Bridge,
secretly cut the cables until the bridge collapsed,
bid on its rebuilding,
hired undocumented Italian, German, and Irish immigrants
and African and Native Americans,
pitted them against each other,
stiffed them on their paychecks.
and bragged about your massive tax deductions!"

"You lousy, two–bit, fear-mongering wimp!
Dance you thin-skinned bully,
DANCE!!"
(P.T. does a Bully Dance.)

How do you make a bully dance?
You put ants in his pants.
You put ants in his pants.
If you meet him on Fifth Ave,
shoot at his feet, like a cartoon Western,
until the coward runs away.
And if his stormy seas turn choppy,
ignore his pleas.
How do you make a bully dance?
You put ants in his pants.
You put ants in his pants.
How do you make a bully dance?
You vote him off the island!

An Honest Man

Come One, Come All to the Cabinet of Curiosities!
See that rarest of animals, near extinction—
a living breathing Honest Man!

Come in! Come in!
There are plenty of seats in the House.

There's just nothing to love
about a principled, honest man.
Nothing to talk about.
Nothing to get the blood boiling.
Nothing sexy.
Nothing to bribe.
Nothing to sell.

The public claimed to be upset by my lying humbugs
but what they really hated was when I, P.T. Barnum,
monster master of the sideshow,
stopped making up stories
and ran for office as a principled ordinary man.

That's right, before I was an apparition in a ghost shirt,
I served in the Connecticut legislature and was mayor of Bridgeport, CT.
Gas lamps on the streets! Hospitals! Museums!
I even gave the skin of my elephant, Jumbo,
to Tufts University for good luck.

Guess who said this
on the occasion of the ratification
of the 13th Amendment ending slavery?
Hint:
It wasn't our 16th President, Abe Lincoln,
or that guy from Hartford, Mark Twain.

A human soul, that God has created, and Christ died for,
is not to be trifled with.
It may tenant the body of a Chinaman, a Turk, an Arab or a Hottentot
– it is still an immortal spirit.

I said that!
I said that on the occasion
of the ratification of the 13th Amendment ending slavery.
And by that time, I believed it.

WHO KNEW THAT **COMMON SENSE**
COULD BE SO **COMPLICATED**.

We the people, we the people hold these truths.

Joice. Joice. Joice Heth.
I live in the hereafter eternally damned for fact that desperate to make a fortune,
my first sideshow was Joice Heth.
I bought her act in 1835 from a Kentucky showman.
Joice was a slave.
A blind, crumpled old woman,
she performed as the 161-year-old wet nurse
to the infant George Washington.
Blind and crumpled as she was, she could still try to lift her left arm
while singing hymns to little Georgie.
The crowds loved her. She was charismatic.
But did the audience know what Joice portrayed? What she taught?
She embodied mercifully,
the merciless truth of our parentage as a nation.

(pause)

"You, 45, you are like the ringmasters
who think that pussies long to be whipped!
They think that's the only way
the lions and tigers will satisfy their every demand."

A real ringmaster never lets the lions loose on the crowds.
A real ringmaster makes sure that the elephants and the donkeys,
the trapeze artists and snake charmers,
the freaks and songbirds all work together.

In a true circus,
men and women work together.
Everybody has a job.
Everybody gets paid a living wage.

We must think very carefully about who we hire as our ringmaster.
Who knew that common sense could be so complicated?

North, south, east, west
and everywhere in between—
kaleidoscopes of madness!

Erect Peace

I'm planning a new sideshow
and each and every one of you will be cast in it.
It's called *Erect Peace*.
Tsk, tsk,...such naughty thoughts!
That's peace spelled p-e-a-c-e not piece spelled
p-i-e-c-e as in guns or a part of the male anatomy.

People, people, people!
I can see you, even if you can't see me.
These days you are entertaining Me.
Me, the great entertainer, P.T.

I've been watching you
and your fair-haired President
and if I didn't know better I'd think
he was a Civil War reenactor
or the reincarnation of General George Custer, the other blonde,
hoping for a different outcome
in a redo of the Battle of Little Bighorn
played live for big ticket donors
and tweeted worldwide.

People, people, people,
I lived through the Civil War.
I witnessed the Native American genocide.
You don't want to do these things.

The drama of war, how it sells!
How we love to hate each other.
Since Cain and Abel:
the other,
the other,
the enemy—your brother.

Think about it.
If you remove the br from brother
and add an m to other,
you have your mother.
Listen to your mother.
Compassion.
Come with passion to erect peace.

Once upon a time,

I tried to sell a sideshow based on Lysistrata—the play written in 411 BC.
In the late 1800s revivals were all the rage.
This comedy was based on the fact that the end of war
is logically possible if the women on both sides of the conflict
refuse to have sex with their husbands until the men negotiate peace.
Quaint. Who sleeps with their spouse?
Nobody bought tickets. My sideshow was a flop.

The underlying problem: peace is boring!
To be sustainable peace must be energetic, passionate, erect.
We need a fierce and frothy peace—
like heaven on earth.
How else to defeat the lawless drama of war?
We need a peace with rules for civilization so we can rage and debate
about smoking and no-smoking zones but never with exploding cigars.

Erect Peace will be dedicated to Lysistrata.
Whatever you say, in the context of 411 BC,
that gal had balls! I mean brains.

Another Civil War?
Ah, 'fuhgetttabout' it!
Mother Earth is starring in her own disaster movie.
Have you seen the previews?

Poof !

After 146 years, my circus,
by then called Ringling Bros. and Barnum & Bailey Circus,
though still The Greatest Show on Earth, closed.
It takes courage to watch your circus die.

There are new-fangled ideas
about cruelty to animals
and there's trouble at the borders
— cruelty to people.

I dare you to find a good juggler outside of Kazakhstan!

Monster that I was,
in truth, I never was cruel to Jumbo.

In heaven there is no more lying.
At first, I hated that even more than the no-smoking.

IN HEAVEN THERE IS **NO MORE LYING**.
AT FIRST, I HATED THAT EVEN MORE THAN
THE **NO SMOKING**.

The Invisible Circus of the Present Tense

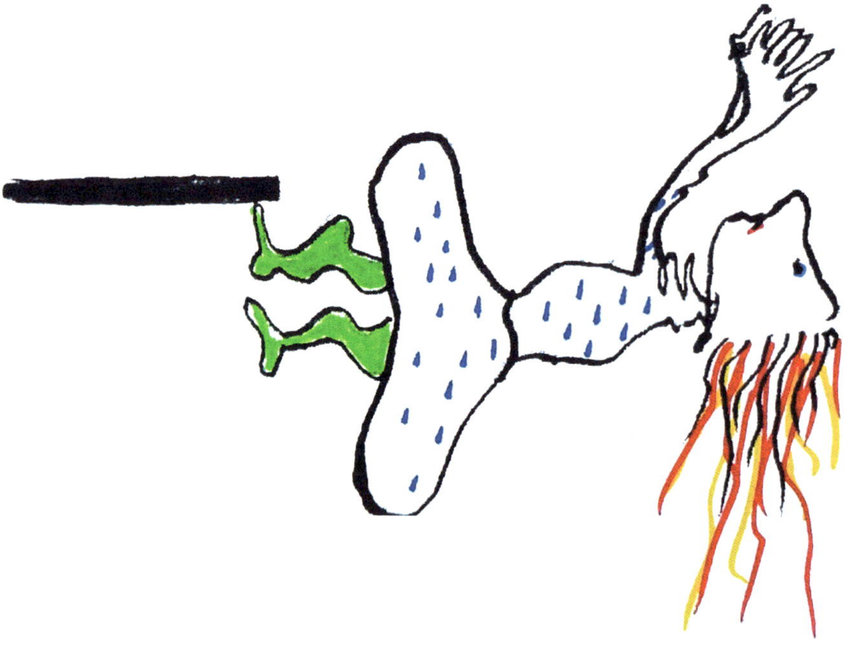

THE INVISIBLE CIRCUS OF THE PRESENT TENSE (2022)

The Ghost of P.T. Barnum appears during the recent pandemic with rules from the old circus that might help us today.

Come one, come, all!
It's so wonderful to zoom back here with you—
whoever you are and wherever you are.

Allow me to introduce myself.
I'm ME, a.k.a, the Ghost of P.T. Barnum—
that 19th-Century circus impresario bizarre
and most famous person in the world
— at your service.

I know, I know, I know,
I almost forgot!
You can't see me yet.

Watch carefully, as I emerge
from a puff of my own cigar smoke.
That's P (as in Present)
T (as in Tense) Barnum

Tada!
A Hoax? A Humbug?

Turns out, heaven is still a no-smoking zone.
On top of that, it's a no-lying zone.
At first, I hated that even more than the no-smoking.

Oh, forgive me!
I nearly forgot.
My pronouns are: me, me, me, me and me.
But enough about me,

this is about you and you and you
and you and me, and me and you.
May I remind you, that each and every one of you is a pre-ghost.
That's right, folks, ghost is your pre-existing condition.
Not mine, at least I have that,
and striped pants, an American bow tie, and an age-appropriate top hat.

May you be living.
May you be living someplace.
May you be living someplace where
the Rule of Law, the Four Noble Truths, the Ten Commandments,
and especially the Golden Rule still hold sway.

And if not, well, don't despair.
We'll always have Paris.

May you be living— not alone,
but with your inner child.
These days, you don't even need to run away to join the circus.

If you get very still and listen,
you can hear the circus within—

Come One! Come All!
To P.T. Barnum's *Invisible Circus of the Present Tense*!

You'll laugh. You'll cry.
You'll have no idea how to fly.
It's the only show in town and it's free!

What could be more thrilling than to fight an enemy you can't see?
Or to finally learn from history?

Prone to amnesia,
we forget the hard parts, the horrific,
so here's a little recent three ring history that affected us all
and changed me, the Great P.T.

April Fool's Day 2020, I swoop down to check out the Big Apple.

New York City, just like I pictured…

I see things that look like circus tents.
But there is no circus.
The streets are empty.
The circus forgot to fold its tents?

What am I seeing? What am I seeing?
These tents are hospitals!
Not since the Civil War have I seen hospital tents in Central Park
I am speechless.
I never thought I, P.T. Barnum, would be speechless.

(coughing)
What's going on?
I'm a ghost!
I thought I was immune.
I can barely smell my grease paint!

I, too, forgot.
We think we are special but this is not the world's first pandemic.
Plague after plague. They come. They go.
We don't learn.
Our children sing, *Ring around the rosie…ashes, ashes we all fall down.*
And they don't even know they are singing a plague song.

Let's begin again.

Come One! Come All!
To *The Invisible Circus of the Present Tense!*
You'll laugh. You'll cry.
You'll have no idea how to fly!
It's the only show in town and it's free!

Trust, not fear, that is the true art of the showman.
I will entertain you with rules from the old circus
that just might help us survive the pandemonium of today.

Rule 1: The Circus Has Rules

Everyone was welcome under my tent.
Everyone was safe under my tent.
I didn't think the audience was stupid.
Susceptible to lies, easily fooled by a good humbug,
but not stupid.

The circus is not ruled by divide and conquer.

Watch carefully!

The underpinning of magic is truth....

To create magic, to discover the timing of the impossible,
circus folks seek truth—
the science of flying through the air, the rigors of illusion.
Their lives depend on it.

The lion tamer puts his head in the lion's mouth just for you.
And why?
So you can practice courage.

Rule 2: The Underpinning of Magic is Truth.

Let's examine the high wire act.
Watch our trapeze artist fly through the air with the greatest of ease.
It's not easy at all.
Our hearts soar!

If a trapeze artist misses the clutch and plummets to the sawdust—
Oh, no! They're hurt! This is real life.
What does a ringmaster do?

A fear-mongering ringmaster might deal with reality this way:
"You did not see what you just saw.
And if you say what you just saw, you're out of here!
What you just saw never happened.
If you say what you just saw, I will hunt you down.
You did not see what you just saw."

NO!
A true ringmaster makes everything stop.
Expert medical care arrives to care for our fallen.
We had doctors on staff—the very best.

We watch in silent separated suspense
as the stagehands test the rigging,
test the nets, test the timing.
It's dangerous. It's complicated.
What went wrong? What will happen next?
Will the show go on? Is this the show?

When it's safe again,
The ringmaster shouts, "Let the flying begin!"
The audience explodes in applause
at the spine-tingling terror and joy of the present tense.

In the circus we are one family
and like a real family,
we face the freak in each other,
especially at holidays.

See a working family, on the ground and in the air.
Imagination is the muse of every worker.

I trust my circus family. Why wouldn't I trust them?
They are making me rich!
Why wouldn't I keep them happy?
Why do people have such a problem making other people happy?

Rule 3: When the Workers Thrive, the Circus Survives

I know. I know, I know.
The ringmaster makes more than the lion tamer,
who makes more than the bare back rider,
who makes more than the organ grinder,
who makes more than the sanitation crew,
who make more than the seamstresses.

But every worker knows they are essential and
can live on the earnings of one job they get respect for
and still hold onto the dream of becoming ringmaster rich,
a star of the trapeze or a strongman chained to a chair in a side-show.

Together we walk the tightrope of our lives.
Together we thrive and survive.

The circus respects the laws of balance.

You know the act that flips teacups on top of each other up and up and up and up?
The stack goes up and up and up until the stack begins to wobble.
And then, bang!
The whole shebang, cups and saucers, crashes!
We gasp in disappointment and delight.
Why? Because we have watched accumulations of excess rebalance.
The top-heavy topples.

The circus respects the laws of gravity.

Hey, stir crazy are you?
Are you lucky enough to have a home,
and then be stuck at home and stir crazy?
Move from one room to another.
Or if you only have one room,
from one side of the room to the other side.
Imagine you've gone to Paris.
Or your favorite beach or mountaintop.

Drop the remote! Drop the ennui and join me.
Drop your phone and start stirring!

Stir the soup and share it.
We make a meal with what we have,
and if we have, we share it.

Stir for the Golden Rule. Stir for hazard pay. Stir for vaccinations.

Stir for voting rights.
Stir for a Senator with a Roman hairdo to walk for one month
in the shoes of a single parent with four children and three minimum wage jobs.
And then ask that lawmaker, "What would actual Jesus do?"

Stir the soup in the three-ring kitchens of your kindness.
As you share your soup, as you care for those who have fallen,
I begin to smell the greasepaint of the present tense.

What good is it to be speechless and afraid?
It's the vacuum of terror into which fascists scream.

Don't be fooled by chaos or entertained by bullies
who promise a fix, a lie, a comforting humbug.
Trust me. I should know.

If you haven't figured it out yet,
this is a redemption story.
For me and for you.
Dare I hope?

A Blank Page.
A Broken Heart.
The blank page of a broken heart asks for poetry.

Rule 4: More Poetry. Less Profiteering.

Hope is the things with feathers.
The poet Emily Dickinson wrote that in my century.

She hardly ever left her bedroom.
If I'd been able to get her to come out of that damn house
and join the circus, I could have made her a star!

Instead, I sold Jenny Lind, the Swedish Nightingale,
as a high-class bird for the masses.
How'd you like them feathers?

I still think of poet Emily Dickinson as the muse of our solitudes.
To me, she will always be a ringmaster of the imagination.

One room, one pen, one poet—
a three-ring circus of hope in one feather.

Oh, Emily…

No matter what happens, the show will go on!

Hurry! Hurry!
Buy that extra bag of popcorn! Or make it at home.
Pull up a chair. It's time for a little fireside chat.

Rule 5: There is no show without an audience.

Here's a Golden Rule conundrum:
You are in my show as much as I am in yours.

I'm watching you.
Bearing witness to your struggles.

I grow in empathy as you create a scene, deny a scene, create science, deny science, create history, deny history, create equality, deny equality, create love, deny love, create peace, deny peace, create racism, deny racism, create cruelty, deny cruelty, create compassion, deny compassion, create war, deny war, create extinction, deny extinction...as you mourn, as you lie, I laugh, I cry.

You could be me. I could be you. It's true.

Do something different in this show.
Surprise me!
Make a better ending.
Better yet, make a better beginning....

The tattooed man!
Captain George Constentenus!
Covered from head to toe with Burmese tattoos of wild animals.

Look into his eyes. He holds a mirror up to you.
His heart breaks, too, and on better days there is joy.
I had imagined you would soften
from looking into the mirror of his eyes.
I was wrong.

I was a salesman, a showman.
I gave you the entertainment you craved.
I confess. I played with your amygdala, your lizard brain.
I fired up fright and flight—
the horror and delight of brains aflame.
But that was entertainment—brute force contained.

Was I the exploiter or the employer of human beings society exiled as freaks?

Was I the only one mean to animals
making them appear to be pets
while some of your forebears shot them from train windows?
Extermination just for fun?

What do we do with all those bullies?

Watch them dance? Ignore them?
Resist them when violence breaks out?
Destroy the bullies and become bullies?
What do we do with all our bullies?

Rule 6: Put Your Amygdala Brain in A Cage.

Put your lizard brain, your lying unfettered rage, in a cage!

Who will you be in the context of your history?
What will you be proud of seven generations from now?
What will be our climate?
What will be the climate of our survival?

I see you and you and you, and you…
Ah, the constitution of a body.
How lucky you are to constitute a living body.
To actually be here.

The good news—all men are created people,
like me, the ghost of a flawed man, played by a flawed woman.

What do I miss most as a ghost?
You.

Pay attention.
Turns out the body politic of the United States of America,
The Greatest Show on Earth,
has an autoimmune disease—
a condition in which the body mistakes its own tissues as foreign and attacks itself.

In the circus of democracy, the audience is the true ringmaster.
Each and every one of us is called to be a cellular ringmaster,
to preserve the tissues, to stop the tearing apart.

If at a cellular level, this virus of lies survives,
the body politic dies.
If you remove a lie, the truth appears as if by magic.

I'm waiting. Waiting for you to take action.

Rule 7: The Golden Rule. There is NO Other. We are each Other.

Have you seen the crowds?
Millions of broken hearts, cellular ringmasters, all
pour into the streets and find the courage to say what they see.

The Invisible Circus of the Present Tense
plays 24 hours a day.
It is never sold out.
Step right up!
Begin again.

Dare I hope?

NOTES ON THE PIECES

First Recipe (2009)

Prompt: Recipes
Premiere: NYC Fringe Festival
Medium: Text and movement.

First Recipe was created for an evening titled *Dances in Funny* produced with Claire Porter for the NYC Fringe. We took on 'the recipe' as our subject of investigation and were joined in thoughtful wackiness with pieces by Karen Eubanks, Susan Thomasson, and Judith Nelson.

Families gather around food.
I grew up in the 1950s and 60s, a time of assimilation in which to become an American in the United States, immigrants and Native Americans were forced to speak English. Children did not learn to speak the many tongues of their forebears---Polish, Italian, German, Gaelic, Yiddish, Spanish, Pequot, and many other indigenous languages. Some of which were lost forever. I observed grandmothers in kitchens, not speaking English, making traditional food. It occurred to me that our family recipes survived intact longer than first languages.

The Chock full o' Nuts Oracle (2017)

Prompt: Memoir, beauty, and aging.
Premiere: Included in *The Fountain of Oldth* by Elena Taurke, The Village Zendo, NYC.
Medium: text and movement.

This is a true story, the memoir of a moment that for me was indelible and better than waterproof mascara. Chock full o'Nuts began in NYC in 1926. The franchise started as a nut shop. During the depression they began roasting coffee and serving lunch. A cup of coffee and a sandwich cost five cents. Some readers may remember their jingle:

> *Chock full o'Nuts is that heavenly coffee,*
> *Heavenly coffee, heavenly coffee.*
> *Chock full o'Nuts is that heavenly coffee,*
> *Better coffee a millionaire's money can't buy.*

Elena Taurke asked me to perform this story in her work, *The Fountain of Oldth*, that addressed issues of beauty and aging with an intergenerational cast of women. Elena's next piece, emerging from her question, "If you could change one thing about your mother, what would it be? And what would that have meant for your life?" was to be performed at Movement Research in NYC but Covid interrupted. The piece was never completed. An artist of wisdom, humor, and courage, Elena passed away in 2022.

An I-Thou Kind of a Guy (2014)

Prompt: *The Namimg of Cats* from *Old Possum's Book of Practical Cats* by T.S. Eliot.
Premiere: The Narrative Assemblage Project, The Dragon's Egg, Ledyard, Conn.
Medium: Text and movement.

I thought *An I-Thou Kind of a Guy* (AKA: *The Cat Dance)* was a 'throw-away' without a life past its first performance, but I have been surprised by the response of audience members. People love their pets and happily share stories of their magic cats and dogs, birds and horses with me.

The Adventures of the Ever-Fragmenting Woman (PG 35) A collection of solos that included Dog Day Ditto (1994) **and Yoga Beach** (1996)

Prompt: Mid-life.
Premiere: The New Dance Series, Belfry Church, Nyack, NY.

Raising two young children and teaching full-time left little space in mind or body to make dances. I could wake up in the middle of the night with concern about two things, not three. I quieted the artist in me and concentrated on being a mother and earning a living teaching and administrating in Manhattanville College's Dance and Theatre Department. Nevertheless, a series of pieces emerged despite my need to sleep more soundly.

PG(35)— i.e., Parental Guidance, 35 years of age— as in the film ratings. The idea is that it takes getting to about 35 to understand the brutality of raising a young family, working full-time (inside and outside the home) at a time when your own parents are aging. These pieces were my first attempts at writing text and were a way to document, observe, digest some of the challenges at this stage of life.

Dog Day Ditto (1994)

Prompt: A car accident
Premiere: The New Dance Series, Belfry Church, Nyack, NY.
Medium: Text, movement, recorded school band.

Dog Day Ditto was inspired by an elementary school ditto sheet —a mimeographed or copied sheet—of questions, with space for the student to make up a story.
In 1994, I survived a serious car accident.
I noticed my son, Jake Appleman's, ditto sheet displayed in the magnet gallery on the fridge. He was to create a story about an injured dog and its trip to the vet. Jake wrote, "The car ran over the dog. The dog lay on the ground thinking of death." My children had put on brave faces but the accident, the totaled car in the driveway, their mother home from work in a neck and arm brace, had terrified them. Jake became a writer and teacher.

Yoga Beach (1996)

Prompt: An incident on Cape Cod.
Premiere: The New Dance Series, Belfry Church, Nyack, NY.
Medium: Text and movement.
Music: Occasional sounds of the sea.
Props: Reclining beach chair, yoga mat, beach bag.
Costume: Knock- off of a Speedo bathing suit, covered by cotton pants and a beach towel

This is another true story. It took place in Massachusetts where 12 percent of the 1500 miles of beaches are available to the public, if you have a car and can find a parking space.

My son, Hale Appleman, now an actor and singer-songwriter, gave me notes after a rehearsal in the living room. He was 11. They included: 1) sharper turn in beginning 2) turn toward audience in bathing suit in underwear 3) move feet more (when upside down in chair) 4) "all of a sudden, she heard" feet move quickly 5) keep spinning on the way out 6) when you make a mistake keep going 7) at the end Ha, Ha, Ha.

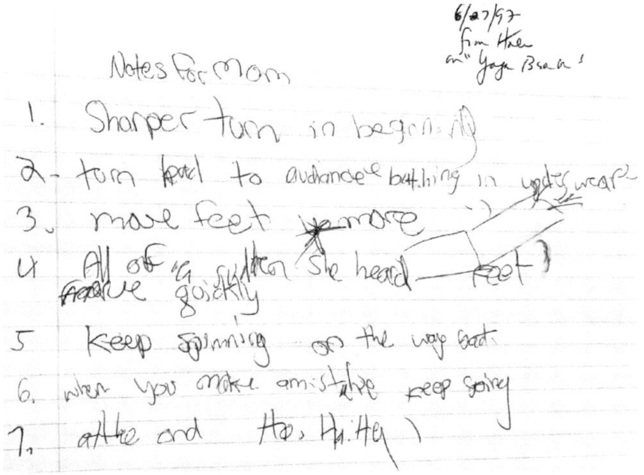
6/27/97
from Hale
on "Yoga Beach"

Notes For Mom
1. Sharper turn in begenning
2- turn to audiance bathing in underwear
3. move feet more
4 All of a sudden She heard — feet move quickly
5 keep spinning on the way back
6. when you make a mistake keep going
7. at the end Ha, Ha. Ha

Although I do not know if the Demi Moore story in this piece is true, despite hearing it on the car radio, I note that she was in the news in 2022, decades later, modeling and selling bathing suits of her own design.

Longtime friend Darcy Casteleiro— writer, comic, teacher, political activist—and I were known to do an improvisation called *Spin and Polish* in which Darcy posed trenchant
political questions and I danced out the answers. On occasion, I would open for her, and once doing *Yoga Beach* at the Gotham Comedy Club, the owner's response to Darcy was, "Lose the modern dancer."

Letter to Lysistrata (2012)

Prompt: *Lysistrata* by Aristophanes.
Premiere: The Narrative Assemblage Project, The Dragon's Egg, Ledyard, Conn.
Medium: Text and movement.
Works Cited: Aristophanes. *Lysistrata.* A Signet Classic, translated by Douglas Parker, 1964.
Story of Noble's obituary: *https://en.wikipedia.org/wiki/Alfred_Nobel*

A Rant.
Lysistrata would have been proud of the MeToo movement which now faces political backlash so severe women may be forced again into servitude, our rights as human beings and members of civil society extinguished. *Lysistrata* is still performed worldwide. Spike Lee's 2015 movie *Chi-Raq* is a contemporary interpretation set in Chicago. Is a strong woman always to be a subject for derision? How do we broker peace?

Why Did Sarah Bernhardt Sleep in a Coffin? (2018)

Prompt: The poetry of death.
Premiere: The American Dance Guild Festival, Ailey Citigroup Theatre, New York, NY.
Music: Naaz Hooseini
Medium: Text and movement. Including a quote attributed to Bernhardt.
Work Cited: Sarah Bernhardt, *My Double Life: The Memoirs of Sarah Bernhardt*, Project Guttenberg. Release Date: October 1, 2005 [eBook #9100]

I was flummoxed by the Narrative Assemblage prompt.
Then I remembered that the great 19th century actress, Sarah Bernhardt, was said to sleep in a coffin. Death is certain, life is the mystery. I suspect The Divine Miss Sarah slept in her coffin to find the courage to confront the reality of mortality, however much she hoped to wake up in the present tense, delighted with the precious and precarious moments of a brief life. The piece is an ode to some of my beloveds who have passed—my sister, Corinne Fitzgerald; my mother, Elizabeth Tabor Fitzgerald; and my partner's mother, Claire Steinhardt Cunningham.

Setting a Place for Carl (2013)

Prompt: Romeo and Juliet
Premiere: The Narrative Assemblage Project, The Dragon's Egg, Ledyard, Conn.
Medium: Text and Movement.
Work cited: William Shakespeare. *Romeo and Juliet.*

Inspired by and in memory of Elaine Shipman and her love for her partner, Carl.
Esteemed modern dancer and member of the community at the Dragon's Egg, Elaine told us that after her partner, Carl, died, she always set a place for him at the dinner table. This act of love, of reaching out across the void of grief and loss, moved me deeply. What if Romeo and Juliet had survived? What is it to love across family, ethnic, and religious divides?

The Hook of Wonder (2014)

Prompt: *Peter Pan* by J.M. Barrie
Premier: The Narrative Assemblage Project, The Dragon's Egg, Ledyard, Conn.
Medium: Text and movement.
Props: A rocking chair, a cane.
Work cited: Barrie, J.M. *Peter Pan.* Penguin Classics, 2008.

If we find ourselves disconnected from delight, how can we again get caught and carried away on the hook of wonder? Much points to the reality that we are one with the beneficent universe. I don't believe in hell except as we cause its manifestation on earth. See the stars. Read the fairy tales. Get old and observant and remain a beginner filled with curiosity.

Off Her Rocker (2021)

Prompt: A passing thought, a title: *Off Her Rocker.*
Premier: The Grand Manan Museum, Grand Manan Island, Canada.
Props: A rocking chair
Medium: Text and movement.
Projections: Peter Cunningham
Work Cited: *Good House Keeping Magazine*, November 1947.

Off her rocker—meaning she stood up. Or alternatively, she's a bit nutz.
The idea to sit and then spill out of a rocking chair into movement appeared and the title stuck.
A memoir with twists and turns.

Lesley Farlow read an early draft of this book and suggested that the scripts might dance on the page. And Ola De Korne suggested that I write the titles in cursive which I note is no longer taught. It was a strange and marvelous task to write titles in script, remembering my mother's penmanship and her practice of the Palmer method applied to handwritten travel documents in her work as a travel agent.

Slow Dancing Is Easy (2010)

Prompt: A postcard from my son.
Premiere: The American Dance Guild Festival, Ailey Citigroup Theatre, NYC
Medium: Text and movement
Costume: Liz Prince
Music: Wall Matthews

The inspiration for the piece was a post card sent by my son, Jake, when he was 14 and away at summer camp. There was the customary: "the food is lousy, swimming fine, baseball, good." And then: "PS, Slow dancing is easy." In those few words, I knew the revelation of attraction that had befallen him. And of that, we never grow tired.

On Looking Back (2006 and 2018)

Prompt: The myth of Orpheus and Eurydice according to Virgil.
Premiere: Stage (2006): The Narrative Assemblage Project, The Dragon's Egg, Ledyard, Conn.
Film: Peter Cunningham (2018)
Medium: text, film.
Costume: Liz Prince
Music: Wall Matthews
Sound: Kevin Packard

On Looking Back explores the story of Orpheus and Eurydice from Eurydice's point of view. Orpheus was a star. He was the Frank Sinatra, Bob Dylan, John Lennon, Justin Timberlake, and Jay-Z of Greek mythology. He and his wife Eurydice loved one another. She stepped on a snake and died. The gods offered to bring her back to life. If only men could follow directions.

Watch the Bullies Dance (2017)

Prompt: The 2016 Presidential Election.
Premiere: The American Dance Guild Festival, New York, NY.
Medium: Text and Movement
Costume: Tuxedo jacket, colorful stiped pants, a red, white and blue bow tie, occasional top hat.
Props: Small ornate chair, bunch of dried flowers.
Work cited: *Obituary of P.T. Barnum*, The London Times April 8, 1891.

In 1996, Barnum made his first appearance to 'help' me with a writing assignment to create a conversation between two famous people who never actually met. I was studying for a Masters Degree at Wesleyan University. P.T. had blunt advice for Hillary Clinton about navigating the showbusiness of politics.

He returned in 2016, tired of the fact that heaven was still a no smoking zone and outraged that he'd been compared to candidate and then the 45th POTUS.
Though they are both showmen, P.T. swears that, monster that he was, he had principles. "Trust, not fear, that is the art of the showman. Governing is not show business, it's real life!"

The mask of the Ghost of P.T. Barnum gave me the opportunity to dig into the absurd circus of politics that bludgeoned us daily in the news with the dangers of increasing threats to our democracy.

The Invisible Circus of the Present Tense (2022)

Prompt: The pandemic
Premiere: Solo Arts Heal/The Marsh Theatre, San Francisco, CA. (zoom performance)
Medium: Text, movement, projections.
Projections: Peter Cunningham

When P.T. Barnum bragged about being the most famous person in the world, he probably offended Mark Twain, Queen Victoria, and Abraham Lincoln. He died in 1891. In 2020 quarantined isolation I thought I was free of his visitations, but he reappeared. Along with seeking retribution for his more horrifying humbugs, he offered the hope of rules from the old circus that might help us with the chaos of today.

Ara Fitzgerald, 1985

ACKNOWLEDGEMENTS

None of us creates a solo alone.

My collaborators on this book:
Peter Cunningham who suggested it and lived with its process.
Ola DeKorne for brilliant book designs.

Gratitude for their wise feedback, encouragement, and close readings:
Darcy Casteleiro, Alison Hawthrone Deming, Lesley Farlow, Heather Harpham, Lu Olkowski, Dian Parker, Monica Valenti, and Elizabeth Zimmer.

Deep Bows to Marya Ursin for The Narrative Assemblage Project/The Dragon's Egg.
Six of the scripts were inspired by prompts given by Marya for the Narrative Assemblage Project at The Dragon's Egg in Ledyard, CT. I, among many other artists, have been blessed by Marya Ursin and Dan Potter's generosity in providing a space for artistic residencies in a magical building with an open dance floor, an indoor swing, a wall of windows welcoming sunlight and seaside fog into a structure with rafters the colors of a bright rainbow. The air is different in here.

For creative process, inspiration, support, and community:
Michael Posnick, Lesley Countryman, Martha Moore, Wall Matthews, Wendy Mathews, Katherine Kramer, Clare Byrne, Cassie Tunick, Alice Teirstein, Liz Prince, Deborah Ivry, Karen Steinmetz, Deborah Tacon, Sara Kiesel, Gina King, Vicky Forster, Pat Catterson, Marta Renzi, Jo Shaw, Sandra Laub,Gloria McLean, Lance Westergard, Sue Bernhard, Tina Croll, Mary Seidman, Kaoru Ikeda, Anabella Lenzu, Columbine Macher, Dyane Harvey Salaam, MJ Edwards, Carly Fleet, John Edwards, Alexis Phillips, Stuart Pimsler, Suzanne Costello, Mark DeGarmo, Jan Hanvik, Jaune Evans, Enkyo Pat O'Hara, Joshin Barbara O'Hara, Eve Marko, Bernie Glassman, Geoff Shoun O'Keefe, Claire Porter, Joan Durkee, Karen Eubanks, Susan Thomasson, Judith Nelson, Elaine Shipman, Karel and Anneke Bakker, Ruth Barnes, Kari Christensen, Art Bridgman, Myrna Packer, Rebecca Stenn, Sara Juli, Greta Levart, Randy Williams, Hannah Fox, Shawn Bible, Cathleen Cahill, Charlotte Currier, Ellen Novack, Carey Perloff, Polly Pen, Andre Ernotte, Julia Gleich, Jason Andrew, Gabri Christa, Erin Martin, Denman Maroney, Naaz Hooseini, Mike Lounsbery, Sue Fleishaker,Gregory Bain, Lisa Nelson, Lois Welk, Mary Ann Smith, Charles Hayward, Yung Yung Tsuai, Chinabear, Lee Connor, Vicky Tansey, Saluka, Libby Nye, Margie Beals, Sarah Stackhouse, Ping Chong, Meredith Monk, Paul Zimet, Ellen Maddow, Harry Streep, Maeve Kinkead, Katherine Stossel, Kathy Posin, Joel Beard, Ted Striggles, Deborah Sale, David White, Stephen Karcher, Colette Gilbert, Richard Bull, Cynthia Novack, Pedro Alejandro, Jane Downes, Cecil McKinnon, Gerry Bamman, Gary Tacon, Cordette Grimsey, Fred Grimsey, Claudia Aldana Flores, Emily Mann, J.Raneli, Karolann McDonald, Eileen Robbins, Leslie Ayvazian, Karen Bean, David Dorfman, George Russell, Beth Soll, Lee Oliphant, Steve Kay, David Jaffe, Kato McNickle, David Eliet, Peter Woodin, Blake Allison, Laurie Cameron, Joe Clark, Rusty Clark, Larry Arrick, Barbara Damashek, Norman Renee, George Lane, Robin Schmidt, David Berry, Julia Lee Barclay-Morton, Barbara Barrie, Lotte Goslar, and the many dance and theatre students with whom I have shared a classroom.

Gratitude to my beloved extended families: The Applemans, Fitzgeralds, Cunninghams, …rs, Martinsons, Butlers, Streeters and Tabors.

Mentors: It is a blessing to have had mentors Martha Myers and Daniel Nagrin.

And finally, thank you to the stages:
Dance Theater Workshop (now NY Live Arts), Solo Arts Heal/The Marsh Theatre San Francisco; Triskelion, the 92 St. Y, Eden's Expressway, Ailey Citigroup Theatre, The Grand Manan Museum, The Grand Manan Gallery, Mark DeGarmo/Salon, The Village Zendo, Manhattanville College, Connecticut College, The Baltimore Theatre Project, The Dance Place Washington, DC; Pascal Rioult Dance Center, Grinnell College, The Dragon's Egg, Primrose Retreat Center, Wisconsin; University of Wisconsin Milwaukee, The Production Company, The Gotham Comedy Club, University Settlement, Brooklyn Performance Combine, The Yard, The Knitting Factory, Dixon Place, The Construction Company, Theatre for the New City, White River Gallery, Zen Center of Chicago, WET, The National Theater Institute, Dance Now, The National Shakespeare Conservatory, Trinity Square Conservtory, The New Dance Series at the Belfry Church, Ko Festival, Zen Peacemakers International, Edinburgh Festival Fringe, NYC Fringe Festival, Rutgers Church Events. Film: Trail Dance Festival, Rogue Dancer Festival, Delaware County Film Festival, American Dance Festival Movies by Movers.

PRAISE FOR **SLOW DANCING IS EASY**

Ara's writings and drawings are wonderful- poetic, wise, heartfelt, surprising, sad, fanciful, restless, many layered, playful, dark. Not full of irony and smirky cleverness, they are so not what is 'in,' and that is what I love about them. Though she claims to not be that much Irish, inside all her whimsical musings, there is always a dark cloud over her head.

-PAT CATTERSON, *Choreographer, writer, teacher.*

Ara's work is brilliant on many levels... smart, moving, beautifully structured and always offers a kernel of humor. This is solo work at its best.

-JOANNA MENDL SHAW, *Choreographer, director of The Equus Projects*

Ara's original and unique narrative dance performances are visually beautiful, thought provoking, emotionally nuanced and politically aware.

-MJ EDWARDS, *Curator/director Grand Manan Museum*

Ara Fitzgerald's work is quirky and profound in the same moment. I find myself laughing with abandon in one section and then quickly brought to a place of exquisite tenderness in the next.

-REBECCA STENN, *Choreographer, artist, faculty The New School*

Slow Dancing is Easy is a surprising gift, vital medicine, rich dharma, and a tweaking of my ears. This beautiful book, should be sung aloud and slowly danced, shared after dinner and in the dark, to be performed with wild eyes smiling with those we love.

-GEOFF SHOUN O'KEEFE, *Executive Director Zen Peacemakers*